EDENS I HAVE
KNOWN AND LOVED

A SAILING GUIDE
TO 50 OF MY FAVORITE
PARADISES IN THE
SEVEN SEAS

BY

MIKE RILEY

FOREWORD

In almost every port in the world, strangers always ask where my favorite places are. Where in all the world, did we think was the best eden, bar none. Where was perfection. For a long time I always replied, "Right here." In the belief that if you can't be in the port you love, love the port you are in. It never went over very well. Inquiring minds really wanted to know.

In an attempt at education, I explained that different ports are our favorites for different reasons. Some were down right gorgeous. Others had an abundance of good restaurants or instilled a sense of peace. Still others were a fisherman's paradise. None of my favorite paradises had everything.

For a while, I became surly and when asked repeatedly where were my favorites, I replied, "Anywhere you aren't!" Karen always gave me a disappointed look as only she can, so I had to stop saying that.

They are not all the same, you know, echos of each other. These paradises vary as widely, as widely as the personalities of the seekers of edens. You might even find that faced with so many genuine paradises, your definition of eden might change. I hope that some day you might be able to visit all of these. It won't be easy. I am on my third circumnavigation and still have many places to visit. Best I can say is time is a wasting so better get cracking. I should be able to say that in seagoing lingo, sorry!

Anyway, here, finally, is the answer to all those questions, to all those people, through out the years. Here is Mike Riley's Ports of Perfection, Reefs of Rightness, Edens of Excellence. Now, if only those same people ask me where the best places are, I can sell them this book and save us both a lot of time! So, here in no particular order are my favorite Edens! Finally, you will have your answer!

Mike Riley
San Juanico
Baja California
Mexico
Pacific Ocean

TABLE OF CONTENTS

HOLE IN THE WALL
WESSEL ISLANDS
ARAFURA SEA

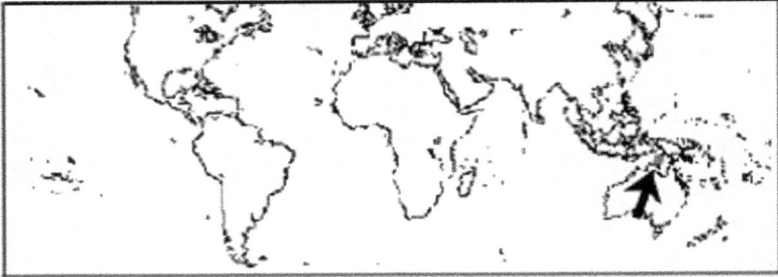

The Hole in the Wall is a short cut through the Wessel Group of Islands that projects a hundred miles northward from the Western edge of the Gulf of Carpentaria in the Northern Territories of Australia. They are a wild group of islands that were never civilized. Not that there is anyone there to civilize anyway. They are peopled by kangaroos and wallabies but ignored by man.

The tidal flows of the entire Pacific and Indian Oceans compete with each other trying to get through this one little pass, a break in the long line of solid islands. Remember Niagara Falls? Ha! If you want to see water really twisted and torn apart, you will have to travel to the ends of the earth, you will have to go to Hole in the Wall.

As you approach the Wessel group from the east with the full force of the trades on your back blowing you towards a seemingly solid string of cliffs hundreds of feet high, your heart is in your throat and your palms are sweaty. Even from a mile away your eyes ache from staring, hoping for proof that you are not going to crash your vessel against the end of the world. Finally, at last, there it is, the pass! But something is wrong! There must be a storm or something ahead as all of the water is flying around, jumping up and down, being tortured by evil spirits; perhaps a volcanic eruption is taking place and the entire ocean is being boiled! And you have to take you boat through this pass, this only Hole in a 100 miles of cliffs! But, of course, you have done your homework and just as you arrive the tide goes slack and you squeeze through dodging this way and that around the larger rocks and emerge, finally, on the other side and paradise!

Beautiful long white sand beaches stretch for miles along bays that have waters as quiet as the grave you so recently thought you were doomed to inhabit. As you walk along the beaches, huge fish swim up, staring at you, like they have never seen a tree that walked before. Little wallabies peek at you from behind trees and then courage evaporated, hop madly away. A sense of peace settles down on you, in this far off place. You are now in the never-never. A section of Australia where time doesn't exist. Enjoy it. Soon enough you will continue your seemingly endless west bound path. Some say that it is the contrast between the terror of the Hole in the Wall and the peace of the lee of the Wessels that account for the sense of well being in the never-never. I don't think so. The world is full of strange and exciting places, places far beyond the realm of tourists and the scientific community. Places that can only be reached at the helm of your own boat. Once you find a place like this, don't rush away, like a tourist on a schedule. Stay and enjoy. Stay and develop. Stay in your Eden and be renewed and grow in happiness and bliss. All of the following edens share in this almost mystical ability to renew, to restore, to reinvent tired exhausted sailors.

Cruising the world's oceans can be easier if you stay on the established routes, berth in marinas as much as possible and if forced to anchor, do so only with all your friends anchored close around. Fear is the enemy of adventure. Don't fear. Fear is its own punishment. Seek to grow, seek to be renewed. Seek adventure. Seek Paradise!

RABAUL
EAST NEW BRITAIN
PAPUA NEW GUINEA

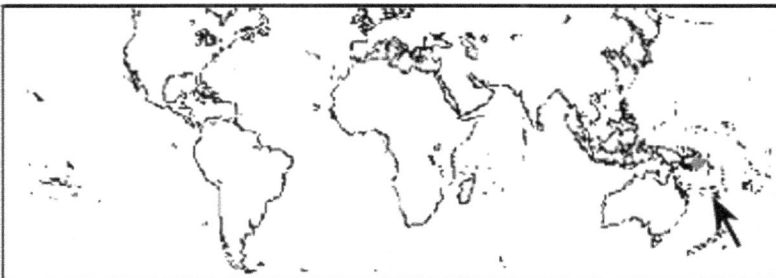

Rabaul was the town most likely to be named the Queen of the South Pacific when it graduated from high school. Its harbor was the caldera of an ancient volcano who's offspring surrounded the bay, looming over the town, quietly smoking in the ominous way of volcanos.

Below the volcanos lay the circular harbor, almost land locked by lush, green almost impenetrable forest. In the middle of the bay the thin, basalt core of the old caldera that soared over the bay. It was the last volcanic effort of a once gigantic eruption.

The Yacht Club was snuggled in an inner part of the bay on the Western side of the harbor. It was a friendly, ramshackle club. The dock was kept from sinking by the heroic efforts of a local handyman and a plethora of rusty nails. The club had a long bar on one side that had seen plenty and bore the memories of wild parties, knife fights and romances carved onto its teak face. Three pool tables were off on the north side. Each table had its adherents as they were so old, the pale green felt channeled the balls into well worn paths if one knew the proper incantations.

The anchorage was 20' to 30' deep and was occupied by cruising boats from every corner of the world. Each had a story to tell and were not reluctant at all to educate a newcomer, for the price of a beer. Every Sunday the Locals had a regatta with homemade sailing models, 6 feet long and decorated with every imaginable rig built of old clothes line, tee shirts, sheets and football jerseys. They were set sailing from just south of the club and then their owners madly raced, on foot, around the circular harbor to greet their boats on the opposite side. A few errant vessels would veer into the anchored yachts off the club. We would urge them on their way with a gentle push on their 8' masts, cheering for "our" boats if they caught up to the leaders.

Rabaul was the center of shell collecting in that part of the world. Fishermen and beachcombers would come into town, paddling their dugouts, to sell a wide variety of shells they had carefully buried in ant hills until they gleamed in their beauty, smell free. Scientists from around the world, dressed in white, topped with pith helmets as protection against the tropical sun, scoured the small stores, seeking to complete their museum's collections.

A weekly ferry came in from Lai and was met by the police. Any rascals on board were turned back and forced to return to the mainland. Rascals sounds like a scamp or a daredevil, doesn't it? Not in Papua New Guinea, it doesn't. These were murderers and slavers and arsonists. Occasionally one would escape the carefully eyes of the police. Then, all hell would break loose until the cops caught him. *Everyone* liked the police in Rabaul!

The best part of Rabaul were the people. Never were there such a vivacious group of wild party goers. They had to be. The town and harbor were surrounded by seven active volcanos, any three of them on every day of the year were on the verge of eruption. The government, daily, published a threat profile, announcing when the next chance of an eruption might be. It was always from one to three days away. One to three days to pack up your life, get on a plane or boat and say goodbye to your recent life. It didn't help that the eruption never came. The tremors under foot and the rumblings from the volcanos just added to the worry. It took a certain kind of person to live and work under such stress. Quick to laugh, always ready to tell or hear a story, they were a great bunch of guys. Few of the expatriates were women. The stress was too great for them. But the few that did live there could teach you a thing or two about partying! One of the favorite pastimes was to hike up 6,000 foot 'Mother' the largest of the volcanos, slide and scramble down into the caldera where steam and sulfur gases escaped from vents everywhere, where rocks were hot to the touch, where occasionally molten lava peaked out of holes in the bottom of the caldera and then subsided, returning to the depths. When that paled, they took their 4 wheel drive jeeps and drove up and down wild rivers and over waterfalls, laughing wildly the whole time. Rabaul was not for the fainthearted.

There were a lot of social clubs in town. Each had their day for a barbeque and movie. As 'yachtsmen' we had a standing invite to the clubs, no fees required. For a dollar, you got a decent piece of steak and a liter of beer. Veggies, dessert and conversation with people who had lived incredible, exciting lives, were free as were the movies.

Lava tubes ran into the base of the volcanos, here, the local musicians played their instruments deep under ground. Occasionally famous bands traveled to Rabaul to play and record their music in the tubes. They told us that these lava tubes had the best acoustics in the world. And late at night, one never had to be worried about being cold. Maybe the beauty of their music recordings was enhanced by the chance of red hot lava running down the tubes at any moment!

During World War II, Rabaul was a major Japanese military port. The Allies developed their practice of leap frog-ing over islands on their way to Japan, mostly because Rabaul was considered too tough a nut to crack. Instead, they sent bombers over the port every day for years to drop huge bombs into the calderas of 'Mother' and her children, hoping to cause an eruption to destroy Rabaul and the Japanese. It never happened. The town and port seemed to live a charmed life.

Rabaul was one of my favorite towns and ports in the Pacific. Unfortunately, on September 19, 1994, two of Mother's children, Tavurvur and Vulcan, erupted burying the town under 25 feet of ash, Pompeii like. Few people died, a result of decades of evacuation drills. Those that did, died of lightning strikes caused by the eruption and generated by the huge cloud of ash that settled over Rabaul. The perfect harbor still remains, but sadly, only a few people stayed to eke out a living there.

I visited Rabaul in 1986 when it was still a bustling town with an incredible market. A carton of cigarettes cost $2 American, but no one would trade for them. The locals wanted leaf tobacco, a 3' leaf, cut right from the plant and dried in the shade for 3 months would buy you a month's worth of veggies on the out islands. Fruits were a dozen for 10 cents, exquisite carvings of sealife a dollar apiece.

I was rebuilding the insides of my boat, the local lumber merchant left my wood in the rafters of the boat house at the beginning of the club dock. I went and paid him on the following day- 2 bucks for a 8" by 1½ by 10' piece of teak.

Rabaul was one of my most favorite ports in all the world, back then. It is being rebuilt now as I write. The lure of the world's most perfect harbor was too tempting to resist. The Island's government, of course, is staying far away, but that just increases the lure! One hotel went in and dug its property out. It is kind of strange, dark and eerie, what with being surrounded by tall granular walls of solid, compacted volcanic ash!

Mother and her children still smoke, daily. Rumblings, below your feet are still felt. But more often than not they are the rumblings of new construction. Slowly Rabaul is being rebuilt.

If you are ever in the area, don't miss Rabaul. It will give you an appreciation of the power of nature and the persistence of Man. And, yes, if you want to get rid of your space consuming shell collections, they will still buy them there.

ANT ATOLL
OFF POHNPEI
EASTERN CAROLINES

Ant is the most beautiful atoll in the world, bar none. It is only 10 miles off of Pohnpei, a huge high island much like Tahiti was 70 years ago. You would think that Ant would be over run with tourists, jet skis and beer salesmen, wouldn't you? It isn't so. Ant remains a undisturbed paradise.

The undulating, snake like entrance is the first indication of Ant's differences. The water is crystal clear and the jagged sides of the entrance reef are enough to require all of the crew's attention. So it isn't until the boat clears the narrow pass that you have a chance to look around. The only island with protection from the easterly trade winds, lies to starboard. Not a big motu but it makes up for its size by its exquisiteness. Coconut Palms line the beach and lean over the brilliantly white sand beach until their leaves are just inches from the water. Other palms grow only to 6' in height but yield drinking nuts that will put you off soft drinks for the rest of your life. Underwater, huge Giant Clams, a meter across, decorate the bottom with all their myriads of colors and dark alluring interiors. The lagoon is full of tropical fish of every description and all of them want to stare at you through your facemask swimming inches away from you.

I visited Ant Atoll in 1985. After the wild party island of Pohnpei, I was ready for some peace and quiet. Ant supplied both. By some miracle, Ant is still unspoiled to this day. I supposed it is because everyone who goes there is so awed by its beauty, they pick up after themselves and leave it a better place.

Ant is one of those places that change you. Just by breathing the air, your body and mind alter until a new better, happier person emerges. No one knows why. It is just one of those things. Many people refuse to enter the pass, preferring to remain the way they are. Ant is a litmus test to determine if you are a seeker or a stay-the-same-er. What kind of person are you? One that appreciates beauty or likes to prey on it? Either way, not to worry. Ant won't hurt you. But if you are a seeker, Ant should definitely be on your 'must' list! The new you will thank you!

CHAGOS
BRITISH POSSESSION
300 MILES SOUTH OF THE MALDIVES

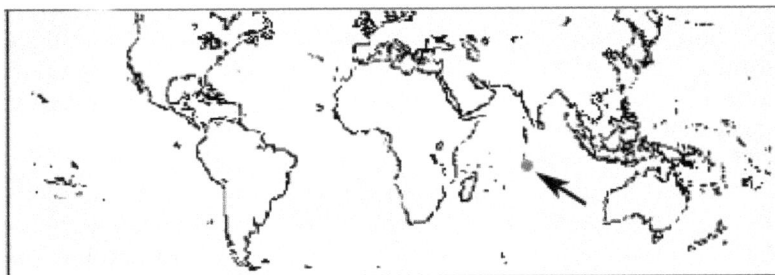

The Chagos Archipelago almost comes up to the beauty of Ant Atoll. For years they were a stopping point for cruising boats heading west. Then, as sailors stopped racing around the world and stopped to smell the roses, they spent more time in Chagos. By the 1990's many Cruisers spent 4 months in Thailand and 8 months in Chagos, year after year. It is such a paradise!

You were allowed to stop and anchor in three different lagoons, each with many islands, or motus as islands mounted on the outer lagoon reef are called, but you had to swear never to sleep on shore or to build structures there. The islands used to be inhabited, but once the Brits, who own the islands, got a chance to rent the largest atoll, Diego Garcia, to the Americans for a cool million a day to use as a military base, life changed for the inhabitants. The Americans didn't want any local people holding demonstrations saying, no nukes in Chagos. The Brits said, No Problem, and simply displaced a few hundred people and sent them to Mauritius in the early 1970's. The last thing they wanted now was a bunch of yachties playing Swiss Family Robinson and taking up residence and carrying no-nuke signs.

Those first few years were heavenly. The islands were cultivated like country clubs. Houses still had beds in them and even sheets on the beds. Fruit and hammocks abounded. The islands were covered in trimmed green grass, allowing the trades to blow across the land keeping the bugs down. But as soon as the locals were gone, slowly nature fought back. Weeds proliferated, houses fell down, insects dominated and the islands were choked with growth. Not just plant life. With no one to eat the fish, to hunt the coconut crabs, to pick the breadfruit, to harvest the coconuts, the islands became wild paradises after the first abandoned decade. The few hearty sailors who ventured across seas in those days, spread stories of the wonders of Chagos, stories of a hidden paradise in the middle of the Indian. Most scoffed that such a place could exist. But every year a few others wandered off the beaten path and discovered islands beautiful, beyond belief. In the years following, yachties built paths and trails to the various fruit trees, built tree forts carefully hidden from the eyes of passing British ships, and had world famous wild parties on the beach. Chagos became the most famous Shangri-La in the cruising world.

By the new Millennium, 100 cruising boats a year visited the Archipelagos and the Brits started charging money to stay to discourage overuse and to remind people exactly whose islands these were. By 2010, stays were limited to 30 days, fees were 700 bucks which had to be pre-paid, and the islands started to revert back to nature once again.

In those early days, it was a paradise indeed, but it is still more than worthy for a visit, if only as a wild shrine for the many circumnavigators who had passed that way before and to eat fish and coconut crabs. They are so plentiful, it is a real danger walking around the islands in poor light. The crabs can easily lop off a toe or two before you can react to something under that palm leaf.

I visited Chagos many times. First in 1978, just a few years after the locals were banished. Last time in 2001. Each time I visited I never left until all food stuffs on board were eaten, propane burnt, diesel dangerously low. How could I, or anyone, voluntarily depart paradise? It really is, even today, the number one exotic cruising destination on earth for those cruisers who like nature as it once was.

HANALEI BAY AND THE NA PALI
KAUAI, HAWAII

Kauai never accepted tourists in the way of Oahu and Maui. Instead, they tried to hold them at arm's length, banning construction of buildings taller than the tallest coconut tree. As a result, Kauai is a beautiful island, and the most beautiful part is the Na Pali Coast. This is on the Northern part of the Island. The coastal road that almost circles the Island is stopped from circumnavigating by the steep, rocky ridges and lush valleys of the Na Pali. These valleys used to shelter thousands of ancient Hawaiians, but times have changed. Now only freedom seekers nudists and explorers climb the 18, 4000' foot ridges, and descend the 19 sea level valleys to reach the heart of the Na Pali. There where ancient, gigantic fruit trees still grow, there where there are no police, no government, no stores, no civilization save what you can form yourself. The soil in the valleys is so fertile that if you drop a tomato seed on the ground, a month later you are eating your own tomatos. The beautiful beaches are gorgeous to sit on, but they lack shelter for any kind of boat, save a Hobie cat or a local dugout canoe. Even then it is sometimes so rough that landing in any kind of craft is impossible. Sometimes they bring helicopters in. But there are only a handful of days a year calm enough to land.

Hanalei lies at the end of the coastal road and the start of the Na Pali coast. There, in behind the Casuarinas trees, which sing with enchanting music as the wind rushes through their branches, is a perfect anchorage. Coral reefs grow out from the points, keeping invading swells from reaching the anchored boats. Ashore there is a Laundromat, a grocery store, a post office and a bar. What more could a sailor want? This was long before e-mail, or even sat-nav. Post Offices were all important, especially for those hundreds who were sheltering behind Na Pali's looming cliffs.

Living is easy anchored there, finish cooking, toss the pans overboard with a line tied to the handle and let the small puffer fish scrape every morsel of food off the plates. Back then as a single-handed, I remember burning pans so badly that I thought I would have to throw them away. However, overnight, the puffer fish with their parrot like beaks, scraped every bit of crust until the pan shone. Ashore, little fresh water streams wander down from the mountains. On the beach, sailors leap laughingly into deep pools of the streams and wash the salt off their bodies with the natural soap of beehive ginger blossoms, picked from the streams edge. Out on the reef, lobsters and fish abound in God's refrigerator, waiting for the next full moon party. (Editor's note: Yes you can use ginger flowers for soap. Check out Mike Riley's "How to Thrive on Tropical Deserted Island." Available at Amazon.com)

Nowadays, hotels sit on cliffs, golf courses dot land where cane used to grow, but the harbor remains the same. The wind still whistles through the pines and Hanalei still weaves dreams into the memories of everyone who anchors in her harbor. They haven't got around to placing moorings and charging for them yet. Now might be a good time to go before one of the most beautiful places on earth is lost forever to cruising boats. And by all means, if you are an adventurer or just a wandering spirit, walk into the Na Pali. It is beautiful beyond belief. Be careful, however. Mail a letter to your parents or children telling then what you are going to do. You might end up staying in paradise for the rest of your life! You'll meet a lot of people up the valleys. They might be your soul mates!

SAN JUANICO
SEA OF CORTEZ, MEXICO

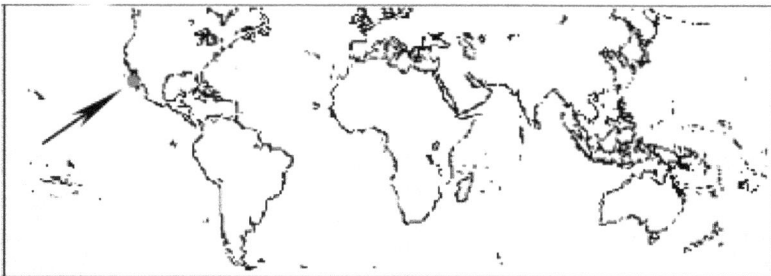

Everyone loves San Juanico. Baja is a wonderful forgotten world of desert and rocks, of a sea abounding with fish and of laughing fellow rovers looking for the next party. If you ever wanted to get away from the world, and never look back, Baja is the place. It is easy to get lost in the Sea of Cortez, the so called, Gulf of California. It's real name is the Sea of Cortez as Cortez was the first white person to cross it, still seeking El Dorado, the lost city of gold.

San Juanico was the first and only place I ever saw lobsters walking around in daylight without a care in the world. Fish, scallops, whales, dolphin, sea lions, everything that lives in the ocean, loves San Juanico. Anchored in the bay, dolphin swim in to serenade us at cocktail time. During the day, humpbacks and Fin Whales jump with joy just outside the bay, ashore sea lions used to bask on the rocks of the point, sailors celebrate escaping from civilization in wild, alcoholic parties ashore under trees bearing plaques declaring that this boat or that visited this bay so many centuries ago. All the anchorages of the Sea of Cortez are great, San Juanico is special. The Sea is an inhospitable place for civilization. There is little water, few roads, death lurks around the corner for any that rely on others to support them. This is a world for the self-reliant.

Along the cliffs ashore are fossils of eons gone by. Deep within the mountains surrounding the bay can be found Apache Tears, knife grade obsidian rocks. Arrowheads made with such a sharp mineral was one reason for the military success of the Apaches. Acute observers can find obsidian arrowheads on the beaches even today. Buried within the cliffs surrounding the bay are crystalline rocks by the thousands. Ages ago, this is where witch doctors came to collect crystals and geodes to give their dreams power as they attempted to cure sick tribe members and to forecast the future. San Juanico is special in all the world.

Islands formed by weird geological processes created a lunar landscape surrounding and amidst in the bay. At night, during a full moon is the best time to appreciate the beauty of the Dali like islands pretending they are lava lamps. No wonder so many full moon parties are held here. Parties full of laughter, fed with lobster, with grouper, with yellowtail and dorado, and with good Mexican beer to wash it all down. Places like San Juanico are where the legends start!

Is San Juanico an eden? You betcha!

FETHIYE
TURKEY
MEDITERRANEAN SEA

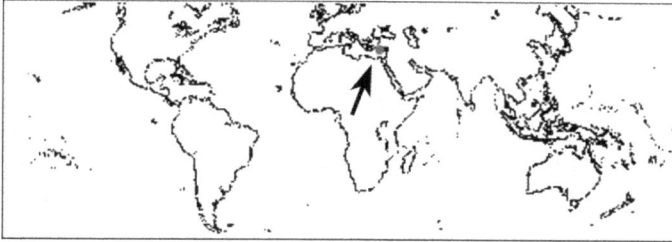

The southern coast of Turkey is full of history. True, the western coast has the remains of Troy and the battlefields of Alexander, but the southern coast contains the ancient cities that were born more than 2500 years ago just before the birth of Christ. History abounds in every port. Unfortunately, most ancient ports have filled in with silt. No longer can you anchor in the same spot as Odysseus, Homer or even St. Paul. Except for one port. Fethiye.

Fethiye is a small town hidden, huddled, below Alp-like mountains that surround the bay. The mountains are so tall that even in summer, snow still graces their peaks. Only the mountains and cliffs can be seen as you approach the entrance. Once through a seemingly solid wall of rock, the bay opens and the town appears to starboard on the south side of the bay.

Anchor in 20 to 30 feet, sandy mud. Go ashore, Turkish Baths are a dollar a go, that is a good exchange seeing it is likely you are going to spend an hour in there soaking the salt out of your skin. Don't worry. They don't care. They have been dealing with sailors since the Phoenicians sailed this way so many millennia ago. The town is alive with bistros offering every different kind of food. Wander through town and find the town market. This is why you came. Not for the Turkish baths, for the market! The place is loaded with veggies and fruits of the very best quality. I still dream of the red pepper that is sold there for pennies. It is the sweetest pepper in the world. Put some on a tomato sandwich and you will glimpse heaven, or at least the pearly gates!

Outside the harbor, are islands and beaches that are some of the best in the Med. Gulags, wood built Turkish pleasure boats, Med Moor throughout the islands and you will do the same. The smell of exotic

19

cooking from their galleys entices you to make friends and soon you will be sitting in their cockpit playing endless games of backgammon. Backgammon is the Turkish National sport and they take it seriously, including the oft forgotten rule that cheating is allowed if the other player doesn't catch it!

Ashore, countless businesses try to get you to sign up to see the ancient ruins. Don't. Wander around yourself. High above the town are the ruins of an old Phoenician fort, free to visit. Just outside of town are stone forts and buildings that date from the age of Alexander. Nowadays, they hold sheep and goats. Everywhere you look, ruins abound. If you make the slightest attempt at interest, soon you will have hundreds of kids guiding you to all the highlights, as long as you play backgammon with them. Ask for a sit down dinner and they will arrange for you to eat at the same table where Mary, the mother of Jesus, ate while on the run after the crucifixion. My wife Karen, pregnant at the time and bone tired after a day of sightseeing, sat on a cot inside of Mary's house. Within 5 minutes she felt resurrected as if she had just enjoyed 8 hours of sleep.

Fethiye is a wonderful, peaceful stop after the hustle and bustle of Greece, Israel and Egypt. Stay for a week and you might end up there for a month. Stay a month and you might spend the season there. Who needs the crowds of Europe when you can wake up every morning in paradise? And it is a paradise. In fact, why not winter there? At least, if you really do like to play backgammon!

ILLE DE VACHE
HAITI
CARIBBEAN SEA

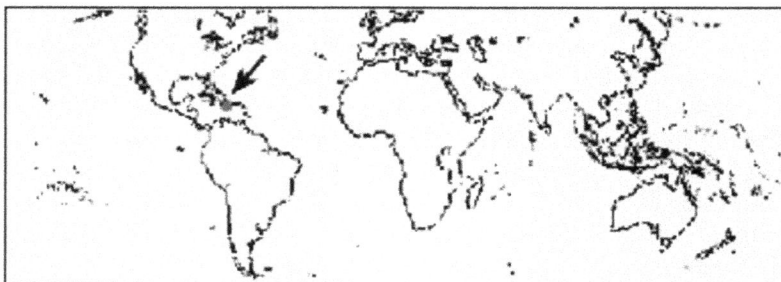

The only "safe" place to stop in Haiti is a little island on the Southwest coast named Ille de Vache. Most of the cows on the 'Island of Cows' are gone now thanks to Haiti's economic troubles, but you don't go to Haiti to eat meat anyway. Ille de Vache is an island of fruit and happiness.

The people are more Polynesian in personality than Caribbean. Every afternoon the girls of the village walk to the well to get water. The boys follow along to ogle and to take turns showing off their prowess as they work the pump. Over across a few hills is the laundry facility, an old WWII gun emplacement which has filled with water. We followed the girls with our load of clothes and were taught how to scrub the material against the rough concrete of the pill box. When the girls tired, they sang songs while picking fruit off close by trees. Fruit was everywhere. It must have been like this in Eden. The boys spend the morning fishing, no that's not right, they spend a hour catching more than enough fish and lobster for the village and spend the rest of the morning showing off doing back flips off of their tiny dugout canoes. The sight of them setting sail out to their fishing grounds with the morning wind is a picture National Geographic can only dream about. The sails are a patchwork of old shirts and dresses mixed with an assortment of old rice bags and a few rare pieces of canvas. They look so much like a flock of discolored sea birds setting out for a day of adventure and mischief. Seeing this you curse yourself that you haven't paid more attention to the sub-routines and white balance of your point and shoot camera. I know, I still curse myself!

Next to the one hotel is a 360° hurricane hole, always of interest to cruisers in the Caribbean. It isn't much of a hotel, what with 6 rooms but a great view of far distant mainland of Haiti. There are several other bays with good protection from the trades, but the one at the NW end of the island is the best, if only for a German who lives on the top of one of the island's hills, who has access to the internet and is glad to share. Others share too, little girls come alongside in a well handled dugout canoes with a potato or papaya as a gift. Older men shared their experience with me as they carve, burn and chip a log into a seagoing canoe. We shared a FEMA tarp, abandoned in the Virgins, that we brought on purpose, knowing that we would stop along the way. They will paddle out to your boat to tell you if the customs boat is coming. If so, you run to the other side of the island and wait for them to go away. Isn't this the way it is supposed to be?

One day the water pump broke. At first we couldn't figure out what they were saying, in their French patois when the boys paddled out to our boat.
"Ze Poomp, it fook oop." (The pump is fucked up. For a couple years after, anything that broke on board Beau Soleil, was 'fook oop!')

We managed to patch it temporarily, and were feasted that night with the best the island had to offer. It wasn't much compared with the South Pacific, but you give what you can, smile a lot, and live with a peaceful conscience.

Is there a better definition of a good life?

PHI PHI DON
THAILAND
BAY OF BENGAL
INDIAN OCEAN

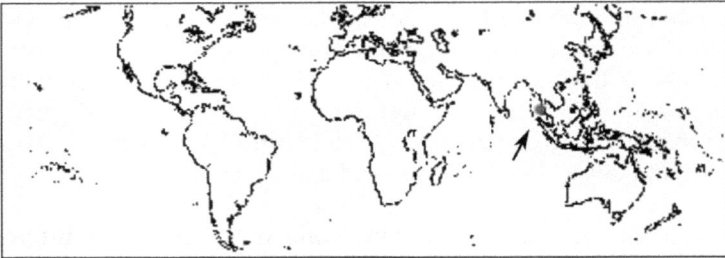

There still exist true Edens in this world. It is true. Quite a few, in fact. Problem is that they are destroyed as fast as they are discovered by a misunderstanding world. Some Edens somehow manage to reinvent themselves, as quick as they are destroyed, like a Phoenix rising renewed from the fire. This is one that might well live forever.

Phi Phi Don is a remarkable island 20 miles off the eastern side of Phuket, a resort island on Thailand's Indian Ocean coast. Phi Phi Don has banned cars, motorcycles , horses, any kind of modern civilization. In their stead are hand drawn carts, beautifully maintained sand paths, and a group of beach restaurants that are unequaled, worldwide.

Thai food is incredible. It really is. The flavors meld together so well, and then as the food is eaten with eyes closed in bliss, the aftertaste explodes throughout your senses taking you to new heights of satisfaction. And all this is yours for a dollar a plate-a heaping plate, a plate so big that they have to put the rice on a separate plate as there isn't enough room! True the beach shacks are rambling, lit by a few dim solar powered lights, the tables are loaded with weird Thai board games to play with while your food is cooked. The crowd is international, all brought together by one common quest:

"The search for the best food in the world."

First the spices are thrown into a red hot pan. The smell that emanates is enough to make the strongest man close his eyes and hold his nose. It is so acrid. It is amazing that such beautiful food can be born from such a aggressive odor. Soon it is gone and more pleasant, mouthwatering aromas waft by, carried by the gentle breezes to your table and then your meal appears. After that you don't care if it is raining, in fact you don't even notice. You won't remember afterwards if music was playing or insects were biting or people were talking. Then, as you eat, the whole world revolves around you and your plate of the best food in the world!

There is more to Phi Phi Don than food. Along the beaches Thai massages are given in tents. Tents because the Thai women use every part of their bodies to stretch every ligament in your body until you can hardly walk afterwards. And I do mean *every* part of their bodies! Nothing little children should watch! The next day, your body is floating on air with totally relaxed muscles, every ache that a physical life of sailing has cursed you with, has disappeared.

Anchored in the harbor, viewing all of this happening ashore along the horseshoe shaped beaches, below the spectacular mountains, a kind of very gentle high creeps into your soul, and stays, echoing back and forth. A high that delves deep into your psyche, giving you, at last, the sense of inner peace you have been looking for, searching for, your entire life. Shangri-La is found! Take a deep breathe. Life is so good. Forget your past. Forget the baggage from your childhood. It is easy to live in the present in such a place like Phi Phi Don!

If you have to move, sail down to Phi Phi Lai, 10 miles south. This is the island where the movie 'The Beach' was filmed. They didn't fake the beach or the lagoon. In fact there is no way film can do it justice. Some things you just have to see for yourself. The place is so wild and so beautiful, no one will live there. How can your ego co-exist with perfection? Well, maybe you can, for a while!

So don't go rushing off from these two islands. The holding is good. The diving beautiful and crystal. The jungle insect free. The people happier than any other on earth! How often do you get to take a deep breath and then release it fully, knowing that you are in a place dedicated to joy?

In fact, stay for the season, and then return for next year. What exactly is the hurry? Are you afraid your dance card won't get filled? Worried someone else might do something you haven't? At the end of it all, St. Peter isn't going to deduct points if you haven't done everything on earth. But he will if you can't look at him with clear, cool eyes that are bathed in an inner joy. An inner joy that can only be developed in paradise!

Years ago, a tsunami destroyed much of Phuket and all of Phi Phi Don. After a day of mourning, everyone got to work and rebuilt the island's restaurants, hotels and infrastructure within a month. You have to respect a people with that much gung ho. Maybe we should send them to New Orleans?

APIA
WESTERN SAMOA
SOUTH PACIFIC

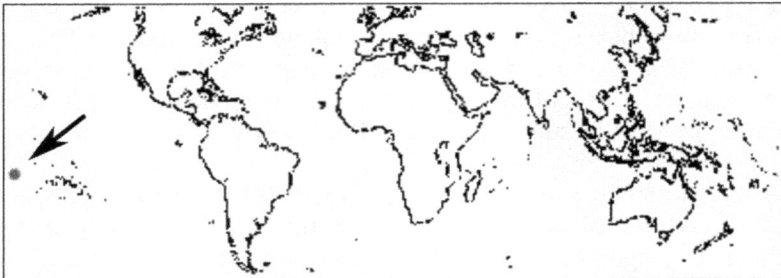

Apia, the capitol of Western Samoa, was my first foreign port of call. You never forget your first. I had banged down from Honolulu in Time Out, a 24 foot Columbia Challenger. I was 23 or so, hard to remember so many years ago. I think it was 1973. I had sailed from California to Hawaii a couple of times, solo, but that was it. I was nearly a total novice.

It was a tough voyage. As usual I was becalmed just north of the Equator. After a couple of days of sitting, drifting between squalls, I tried to row myself across the line, I was sailing engineless as was my wont in those long ago days. It didn't work as I ended up drinking a day's worth of water in an hour. Anyway, I was very glad to drop the hook when I finally arrived. Single handing means you sleep a lot when you arrive, especially before GPS and Sat Nav. I took sextant sights to discover which part of the rather large island of Upolu, I had discovered. Anyway, after clearing in, I slept almost around the clock.

The next morning I awoke to the sounds of horses swimming along the beach and out to and around Time Out. Little boys hung on to their tails, steering them like a rudder, as they were exercised. What a delightful introduction to Samoa! Soon I spotted young ladies swimming on the beach and eyeing my little boat. They had an unusual way of swimming. They went into the water fully clothed, from the neck to the ankles, required behavior by their strict religious upbringing. Once under cover of the water, they disrobed and discreetly frolicked. Once in a while, one would look around the beach carefully, making sure they weren't being observed, then leap out of the water, naked, waving at me madly, screaming, "I like go boat!" Quickly they disappeared under the water and looked around again, shyly, giggling, hoping they hadn't been observed by anyone who knew them. It wasn't hard to entice them aboard. Not at all. It was harder to get rid of them when it was time to explore the island. But that is another story; "The Search For the Wild Wahine" that finally ended when I met Karen. (Editor's note. Check out Mike Riley's "Education of a Falcon" at Amazon.com.)

Ashore Samoa is great. After the obligatory genuflection at the grave of Robert Louis Stevenson, rent a 100cc motorcycle! They are cheap and fun! Everywhere you ride, people are full of smiles and laughter. What a nice group of islands! These are tall islands, smack in the middle of the trades so you have to expect passing showers. No problem, right? You are used to squalls by this time. But what you won't expect is the waterfalls that race down the hillsides and across the streets as you are put-putting along. Hopefully, you still have your girl on the back of your bike as it is easier to utilize the forward wheel as a rudder while aiming up stream hoping to come out close to where the road continues with a bit of extra weight aft.

If your courage wanes or if you end up crashing into a tree, no worries. Passing 1 ton trucks will pick up you, your girl and your bike and deliver you back to Apia for a dollar. In Apia, restaurants abound for every pocketbook. Eat in style at Aggie Grey's (who became famous for fattening up Robin Graham on his circumnavigation on Dove) or join the roughnecks down at the fish and chip shack where the food is wrapped in newspaper! Samoans don't believe in standing in line. Everyone bellies up to the window and shoves their way to the front. If you are a bit lost by all this, no problem, one of the locals will take you under his wing and push you in front of him, using you as a battering ram! Don't get the wrong impression, the crowd is full of laughter and joy. Samoans just don't believe in standing in line. Stay in Apia for a while. You won't stand in line ever again, or if you have to, it will be with a smile remembering your Samoans!

It is easy to sail away. There are so many other islands and countries to explore and hurricane season is approaching. It is so easy to leave. But afterwards, lying in your berth at night you will ask yourself, 'why did I leave so soon.' There is no answer. Paradise lost is the saddest experience of all.

COLON
PANAMA
CARIBBEAN SEA

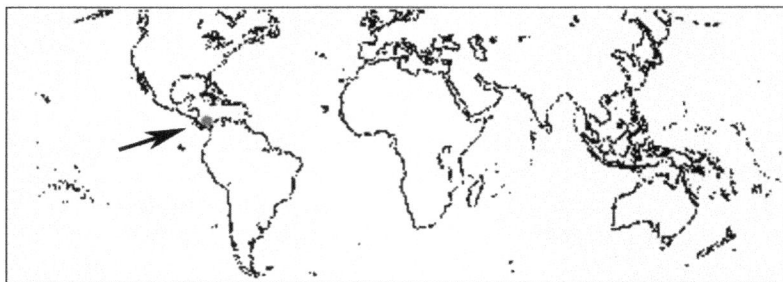

Colon was once and at any time might again become one of the seven deadly cities of the world. There was a time not that long ago that you could be fairly sure of being raped or mugged or simply killed within a half of a mile of your boat. The only safe way to travel was by taxi and only to places that had a team of guards outside the entrance securing the 10 feet of sidewalk between the taxi and the front door. This can be considered a paradise? For who? The devil?

Colon has the second biggest Free Zone in the world. (Second only to Hong Kong.) It is the wildness and joy of the free zone that makes Colon an eden. The Zone is surrounded by forty foot walls topped with barbed wire. The few gates are closely guarded by machine gun toting soldiers. Outside the gates is a wild, barely controlled war zone. Inside the zone is paradise, a paradise for shoppers!

Governments around the world charge businesses inventory taxes on what they are warehousing and waiting to sell. More and more international business are stashing their inventory in places like the Free Zone in Colon where they can be shipped out in hours from one of the centers of shipping in the world and there are no taxes. Thousands of the most famous companies in the world have massive footprints in Colon. What does this mean for us?

We, being in limbo, legally, (we aren't Panamanian, we aren't businessmen, we aren't tourist. The closest thing we might be is sailors waiting to transit the canal.) are allowed to enter the Zone. Legally it is unclear if we are allowed to buy anything there. And we do want to buy things. Taxes make up increasing portions of price of things. On booze, 90% of the cost is taxes. Booze is one of the few things that has gotten cheaper over the years. A liter of VSOP cognac costs $2.93 in the zone. In a store just outside the zone–$73, if you can find it. In New York, $126. It blows the mind, it does. There is little that you can't buy in the Zone. Solar panels, anchors, chain, electronics, outboards, inboards, anything and everything! All for pennies on the dollar! It gets better! If you are anchored in Panama City on the Pacific side, you can pay for something in the Zone and pick it up in their store in Panama City, no questions asked for just 1% increase in cost! This is how the entire world should be organized! Why are shoppers considered cash cows? We shoppers are the engine that makes economies run but we are treated like scum! No longer. We have Colon!

The Free Zone is huge. You might be able to visit it all in a couple of weeks, 10 hours a day. The maps are free but don't have GPS coordinates. You will have to use dead reckoning. I hope you have kept in practice! Where good walking shoes, you'll need them. Don't just go into the flashy stores. The little doors with a little sign are where the real bargains are to be had.

The trick is getting it out of the gates. There isn't any reason why you shouldn't be able to buy anything for your boat as you are exporting it from Panama on your vessel, but this is Colon so there is always mordita, bribes. So we 'smuggle' it out through the gates! It isn't hard.

Everyone has their own tricks. Some stare down the gun toting guards and just walk out. Others wait for a bevy of young women to exit and walk out while the guards' eyes are otherwise occupied. Others go through the rigmarole, to get legal permission (unneeded) to export for a few hundred dollars. In any case, the guards know what you are doing, they just don't care. They will stop you if a gang is active outside the gates. Sometimes they refuse to let you leave until it is safe. Those days are past now, hopefully for good. Whatever you do, if you are heading towards Panama and are thinking about a major purchase, you might want to wait for the free zone. It is a true paradise for the determined shopper. If you are ever in the area, don't miss one of my very favorite edens in all the world, the Colon Free Zone!

LUDERITZ
NAMIBIA
SOUTH ATLANTIC

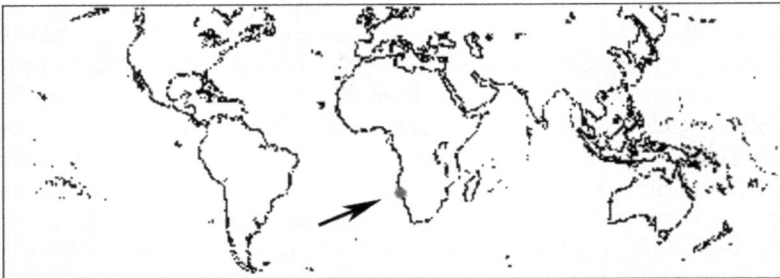

You know about Luderitz, don't you? This is the place in Africa where you walk along the beach and pick up diamonds just laying on the sand. By the way, it is really true. Diamonds are everywhere. I don't know if I have related that Karen, like almost all females, is devotedly addicted to diamonds. The first thing she did after we anchored, was to walk her dog along the beach. She wasn't looking for diamonds, she was just walking her dog, really! That is her story and she is sticking to it. The good, the diamond laden, part of the beach was closed off with wire fence, barb wire, evil guards and machine gun nests. They wouldn't let Karen in. She was heart broken.

She soon realized that the streets were made of a very high quality of quartz. If you squinted your eyes it almost looked like they were streets of diamonds. It wasn't long before she was bringing grocery bags of quartz back to the boat and going through them with her handy, Sherlock Holmes magnifying glass. The tables on board were covered in rock. I found lockers filled with bags of quartz waiting to be examined at sea. When she took a break we wandered about the town. It was more of an oasis, really. Just 4 blocks from the ocean were endless hills of blazing sand. Right out of Hollywood, I was searched for signs of Lawrence of Arabia riding out of the desert, when I lowered my binoculars and realized I had lost my wife. Where was she? Of course, there were foot prints on the sand dunes and Karen was scouring the sands for diamonds. This time she had her magnifying glass stuck in her back pocket. When I finally got her back, along with bags and bags of sand, I put my foot down. No more diamond hunting. She agreed with bowed head, very repentant. The next day the bags of quartz and sand were gone, the tables were clean and Karen was dutifully cooking. All was right with my world. Later, at sea, I discovered the bilges filled with all her collections. Eventually she examined all her raw materials and I got my bilges back. She never did find a diamond but even to this day she always asks when we are returning to Luderitz! And she even gave me a huge magnifying glass for my birthday!

Is your wife looking for a new passion, a new hobby? Is she bored with life? Is she seeking some paradise where the gleam and sparkle will return to her eye? It is an easy answer. Take her to Luderitz. Best to arrive with empty lockers!

SEVEN SISTERS
GRENADA
CARIBBEAN SEA

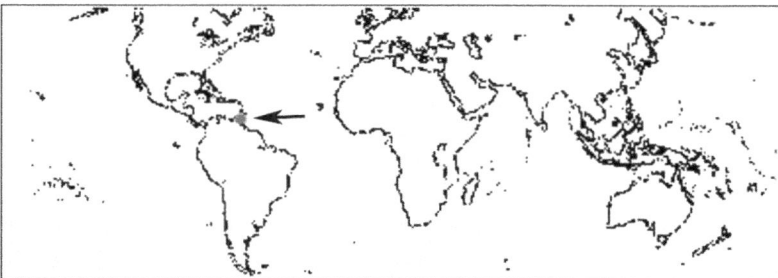

The Seven Sisters are not even on the coast but they are one of the world's most beautiful waterfalls. True they are not as spectacular as Niagara or Victoria nor as well known as the Seven Sacred Pools on Maui but unlike the above they are a paradise. To get there, anchor in any of the many ports of Grenada. There are many. I prefer Hog

Island on the Southwest coast which used to be a pirate hang out but now is just a hideout for yachties who prefer not to go thru the hassle of checking in to the island. (Hog Island held the original Yachtie Full Moon Party and some insist still holds the best. The government routinely shuts Hog Island down, destroys all the camps, play grounds and tree forts. But like the pirates before them, it doesn't take the yachties long to move back in.)

Take local transport to the Seven Sisters. The bus is the cheapest. There isn't a sign on the road. You will have to get the driver or a local to tell you when to get off. No one is there to take your money or to show you the way. Follow the trail, practice your Davy Crockett skills. It isn't difficult. The trail takes you through abandoned plantations including a nutmeg one. There are thousands upon thousands of nutmegs lying on the ground. Don't get too carried away. Karen is still giving hers away 15 years later!

When you get to the pools and have your first swim to wash off the sweat, climb all the way to the seventh pool. The smallest is about 20 feet by 30 feet, the largest, olympic size. All of them are connected by slide like water chutes or diving rocks (not too tall!) The water is crystal clear and delightfully refreshing. Your foremost question will be, "Where are all the people?" Good question. Other than weekends, the Seven Sisters are often abandoned, too bad for the hardworking locals, better luck for us.

The pools are shaded with trees and bushes decorated with an astounding variety of flowers. The aroma as you breathe in after a dive or a slide is incredible as are the butterflies and songbirds flying and singing overhead.

Take off as many clothes as your personality will allow and warm yourself in the tree diffused sunlight. This must have been how Adam and Eve passed the day. Laugh as a butterfly lands on your nose. Drift off in a nap as the cascading water and singing birds take you back to childhood and innocence.

Refresh yourself while washing the salt out of your pores and ready yourself for squalls and storms in distant seas. Before the day is done, before the last bus returns to civilization, say goodbye to your eden. Take a photo is you wish but it can never capture the essence of the Seven Sisters. Are the Seven Sisters an Eden? They certainly pass one of the entrance requirements, you will never forget them for the rest of your life!

KOSRAE
EASTERN CAROLINE ISLANDS
WESTERN PACIFIC

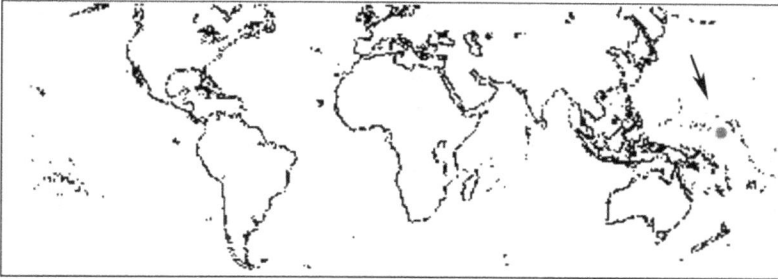

Kosrae was the island of love in the old days in the Pacific before the missionaries came. It was the island where the chiefs sent their daughters or likely wives to study the techniques of love making. It was so famous that even chiefs in Hawaii and Tahiti sent potential wives there before marrying them. Today, away from the main streets, away from the eyes of the church, the old ways still prevail.

In this old world of ours there are edens for everyone. Even singlehanders or women seeking to become better lovers. In many of the Carolines an ancient civilization, older than those on Easter Island and Egypt, once flourished. Remains of their temples still remain on Kosrae and Pohnpei. Their god was the god of physical love. The women on Kosrae have been studying lovemaking since time began. And they are good at it! Beyond belief. It is not my right to share here the techniques they used on me, if I even could, (I was too busy screaming in delight!) but I can encourage those who want to study an ancient subject, to sail off to Kosrae. (Editor's Note. If you really need to know, read some of Mike Riley's fiction books! "The Good, the Bad and the Pirate" and "The Treasures of Cocos Island" both available at Amazon.com and on Kindle.)

The mountains of the island resemble, hell, are identical to a prone woman with her legs slightly apart. Women will have to go through several stages before they are allowed into the main temple between the legs, so to speak. Men can only go so far. It is an island dedicated to teaching women. However, lots of girls are around who want to practice what they have learned!

They do require that you pass rigorous health tests before you are allowed to land including Aids and STDs exams. They require that you sign away your rights before the tests. They are not very pleased at all if you are found to be infected. The least they will do is let you sail off, so make sure you are as clean as a whistle if you plan to stop. I personally know of one singlehander who was threatened with castration before he was released. Be careful!

But if you are seeking a paradise in one of the original meanings of the word, seek no more. It waits for you. All it requires is the nerve to go and lots of stamina! Lots and lots!

MIDDLE PERCY
BARRIER REEF
AUSTRALIA

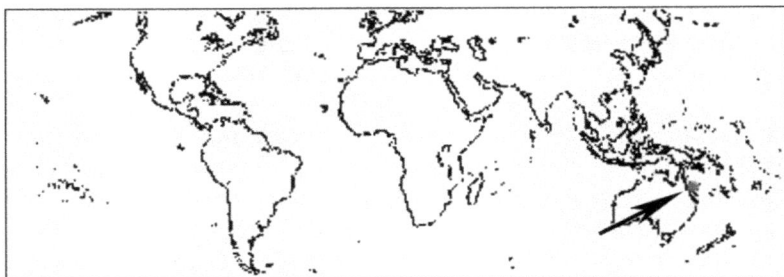

There really are paradises left in the seven seas, I know because I have been to this one three times, each time for a prolonged stay. Middle Percy lays in the southern edge of the Whitsunday Island group, islands well known for their tourism. So, you sail into Percy expecting crowds and jet skis and parachute boats wrapping their tethers around your mast. But it isn't so. Middle Percy is privately owned and they refuse to allow tourists to come within 10 miles. For the cruising yacht it is a different story. They are welcomed with open arms.

The first thing you see on the beach as you anchor off is a bath tub! It is raised up on a throne like platform with pipes leading up to it. On closer inspection, the taps work and in the middle of the day, the water is hot. On a nearby coconut tree is posted a sign, "Yachties, drain the tub after using or it will breed mossies." "Well, if they want me to drain it, I better fill it first!" A bit further up the beach are a couple of shacks. Memories are hung all over them. Signs, decals, flags from cruising boats from all over the world, some of them well over 100 years old, all of them extolling the virtues of Middle Percy. Other signs encourage you to add your contribution to the shacks. Further up the beach is an A frame building with a trading library, consisting of thousands of books, up in the loft above are soft rugs, hammocks and a few Playboys strewn around in case you wondered what this room is for. On one side is a huge open window, displaying the anchorage and your boat down below.

After a few days in heaven, and now that you are clean and all, no doubt you'll want to explore. There are many paths that wander through the heavily wooded island. Take one. Bring your camera. Bring water and a lunch. Maybe dinner, too. Middle Percy is home to 16 different species of butterflies. As you stroll along the path, beautifully hued butterflies soar into flight, startled by your presence. There are so many of them that they obscure the forest, the path, the world. You have no choice. Stand still, or sit on a nearby log and wait for them to calm down. Many of them will come to rest on your head, your arms, your nose. Drink some of your water, eat some of your lunch. Eventually the world will return and you will be able to see and resume walking. Move very slow and only a few thousand will take flight. It is a smallish island but at your enforced snail pace it will take several days to explore all the paths. Try not to laugh in joy at the butterflies. They will fly into your mouth!

On the top of the largest hill, above the forest, is the residence where the owners live, or in their absence, their caretakers. Knock on their door, don't be shy. This isn't an island where shyness should or could exist. Edens don't require shyness as qualification for entry, you know. They will invite you in for tea and a homemade cookie or two and then take you out to the gardens and dig up whatever vegetable you might like to buy and check under nearby ducks for eggs. If you haven't tried duck eggs, do, they are wonderful; big, fresh and great in cakes. They don't make omelets. Sorry! No one knows why they don't gel when cooked. The best eggs of all come from peahens, the consorts of peacocks. They are large eggs that when cooked act like chicken eggs and are 3 times as delicious. See if they have any for sale!

Around the corner by the beach is the harbor, a perfect hurricane anchorage, or would be except for one thing, this part of the Barrier Reef has 20 foot tides. Go in at high tide and you will think you could easily weather a cat 5 hurricane. At low tide however, all the water is gone. Makes for easy clamming but not so good for ocean going monohulls. But don't judge too quickly. In one corner is a well built grid. A dock that you tie off on at high tide, wait for the water to disappear and then clean and paint your bottom. This is Australia, Mate. A bloke does things himself. He doesn't need any blinking boatyard to paint his boat for him! A bit of warning. I tied Beau Soleil up to this grid to replace the cutlass bearing and neglected to tie her up well enough. At low tide, the wind changed and she ever so slowly leaned over, stretching the hawsers I had sent up the hill to near by trees. Slowly she leaned over and ended up on her port side. So if you do use this grid, install a few braces on the water side for a trouble free night!

Need more adventure? Sail over to South Percy, 5 miles away. Anchor off the fabulous white sand beach. Go ashore and read the sign put up by the fish and game committee. "Please shoot the goats for food." The island is over run by goats. There are few trees, especially compared to heavily wooded Middle Percy, and no butterflies. Do your duty and have a barbeque on the beach, preferably during a full moon night with a fleet of laughing fellow rovers. Hint: there is a good hanging tree to bleed the animal just by the big rock. Don't forget to cut out the glands out in the arm and leg pits. Traditionally, the girls dance around the fire as the men cook, but I don't see why it can't be the other way around. Are we in a paradise or not? The rules are different in edens. Different because we become different. More responsible, more caring, more loving. Well, at least Karen became more caring as I barbecued her goat. And she did dance around me almost naked! Hey, I'm sure Eve did too in her Eden! Totally naked!

Islands like Middle Percy are the reason we bought a boat and went cruising in the first place. Isn't it great that perfection exists?

In the interest of total exposure, there are always demons lurking around the gates of heaven. In the Great Barrier Reef, the snakes in eden are sand flies. These buggers have a bite like a rabid dog and the wound is about as infectious. Be sure to bring your Rid or other insect repellant. A caution. Australia isn't ruled by lily livered lawyers. There, insect repellants really do work. Be careful, don't get any in your eyes. Really. Other than that, stay for a while. Take baths. Visit the loft. Enjoy a true eden. Feel yourself relax and forget the argument the two of you had last week. You are happy at last. Laugh with each other, smile in each other's eyes. You will carry a bit of Middle Percy with you when you leave. The day will come when you are sitting on a beautiful beach, enjoying the view and you turn to each other say, "All this place needs is a bathtub!" The two of you will fall to the sand laughing in remembered joy and you will hug each other filled with shared memories.

KASTELLORIZION
GREECE
MEDITERRANEAN SEA

A hundred miles to the east of Rodhos (Rhodes) lies the forgotten little island of Kastellorizion. It is only 3 miles off the southern coast of Turkey and should belong to it. However, it used to be a stronghold of the Knights of St. John so it retained its Greek leanings. According to the treaty between Greece and Turkey, if the population of the island ever falls below 200 people, the island reverts to Turkey who would love to get it. (Turkey and Greece hate each others guts. It started over some girl named Helen! And they are not the kind of people who forget! Plus Greeks hate to play backgammon!) Anyway, when you sail in, you are instantly counted as part of the population which means that some of the locals can take the ferry back to Rodhos to do some shopping. They will try to make you as welcome as they can, to get you to stay as long as you will. (The ferry between Rodhos and Kastellorizion is free to encourage tourism.)

The island is well worth a prolonged visit. It is surrounded by high cliffs except on the north where a perfect little harbor opens up. If you have just come up the Red Sea, this will be your first experience with med mooring. Don't freak out. It is easy. Especially in a little port like Kastellorizion. Not many cruising boats visit, so all the taverna owners come racing out to have you dock in front of their restaurant. All you have to do is throw out a bow or stern anchor, no problem with it digging in. Boats have been med mooring here for 7 millennia. There aren't any bad holding spots left. Ashore, they will tie off your stern line and before you can take a deep breath, there is a table with chairs and an umbrella next to your boat and the bar keep is pouring a free glass of resina. The dark red wine known as resina takes some getting used to, it is true. Be sure to eat olives, goat cheese and the incredible Greek yogurt between each sip and you might survive the first night. And as bad as the resina is, the ouzo is magnificent but for that you pay!

The next morning early, ok, in the afternoon late, take a walk. Go up to the top of the castle (built by the knights of St John, the Knights of Malta's bitter enemies) and gaze with satisfaction at your boat far below and the far off to the north see the coast of Turkey. Continue up the cliffs and pick herbs along the road, growing wild. Chamomile, red clover and peppermint abound.

Allow your gaze to soar to the west and the many islands and countries that are waiting for you that are hidden in the mist. There are few places that can captivate a soul as much as your first Greek Island. Make your first, Kastellorizion. Don't miss it.

PRASLIN
SEYCHELLES
INDIAN OCEAN

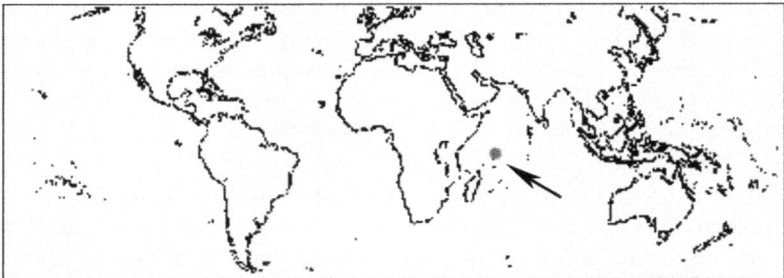

The Seychelles are the only granite islands in the Indian. All the others are basaltic or coral atolls. What that means is that the Seychelles used to be a small continent before it sank, like Atlantis. (Or was Atlantis, if you look at how the Orient was ahead of the west in so many ways, so long ago.) There are still parts of the Seychelles that not only are fascinating but are blessed with incredible beauty. Maybe once, it was the home of an ancient civilization.

The Seychelles have always gone their own way politically. When I first sailed there in 1980, the country was communistic. The next time was in 1992 and they were "enlightened socialistic. But whichever way the country went, Praslin, the northeastern most island, went the other way. They are natural born rebels. When the rest of the country was communistic, Praslin was selling land to rich westerners and running a mini democracy. It is only normal. Praslin is different not only from the Seychelles but also from the rest of the world. Enough so that it is in the running for the site of the original Garden of Eden.

Praslin is the only place in the world where the 'Coco de Mer' will grow. This is the famed double coconut, the coconut that looks like it has two nuts inside one husk. Needless to say, early biologists in the 1800's were greatly frustrated in trying to transplant the palm to China to give supposed extra vigor to aging millionaires. Efforts have continued to this day, but the palm refuses to grow anywhere but Praslin. That has to be a sign of the original eden!

What makes Praslin different? Perhaps the difference is because of the sense of peace that prevails over the island. Other countries have strife, terrorists, criminals, career politicians and lawyers. To be fair, Praslin does too, at least when such people first arrive. But within hours, they are laying on the perfect beaches on one of the world's most perfect islands, content to watch butterflies flitter past their noses, perfect sunsets gracing their evenings and some of the most intriguing conversationalists in the world.

Ancient monks from China spent their lives searching for places of power. Physical locations that fill the body with life force, instilling long life, curing diseases, healing broken minds and hearts. Locations like mountains, lakes or islands. They do exist, these places of power. I believe that Praslin is one. Go there. Find out for yourself. But be prepared to be different from the moment you set foot on the island. It will blow your mind! I know it changed me into a better person. Thank God!

(Places of power cover the earth. I remember one I found in a house in California. It was a very small spot, against a wall and you had to crouch against the wall to enter it. The power that entered me while I was crouched there was an incredible feeling. Of course, once I stood up and moved away, it drained out of me. But while I was there, I was in paradise. No pain, no worries, no sadness no unhappiness. I have often wondered if some psychiatrist's offices are sighted on or around one of these places of power. That would explain why people return for years. Such places are very addictive!)

LIGHTHOUSE REEF
BELIZE
WESTERN CARIBBEAN SEA

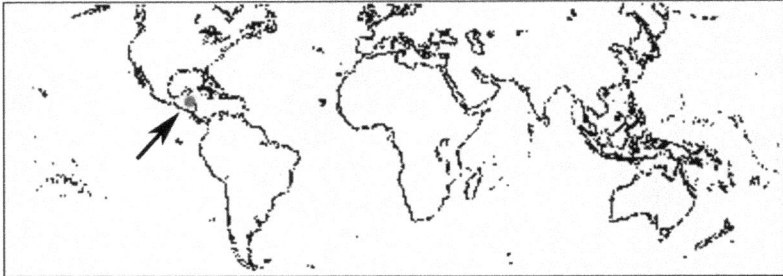

It was inside the lagoon of Lighthouse Reef that man first swam with dolphins, reaching out to them, as an equal and as a reward, were towed all over the lagoon. Lighthouse's reefs contain the first charted Blue Hole. Holes in the middle of a reef that go down thousands of feet and theory has it are interconnected in some astounding way to others around the world. The island rocks with first places. Lighthouse lies at the southern end of the outer string of reefs laying off the Belize coast that run from Mexico almost to Honduras. It is so far off the Belizean coast that authorities rarely visit. It is left for a few adventurous sailors to enjoy an amazing island. If you ever find yourself in the Western Caribbean, you just have to stop. It is like a requirement!

Lighthouse is a true coral atoll with a surrounding reef and a island, Long Island, in the middle. The reef on the western edge is sunken for a football field's length down to 12 feet, just enough to sneak in on a quiet day. Once inside, look! Paradise! Close to the island the water is 10 feet deep and it is like you are in the Bahamas again and the water is as clear as the air. Fish swim this way and that and there is no need for an underwater camera, not in water that clear.

There is always a snake in every paradise. The snakes in Lighthouse are the northerly fronts that come roaring down from Canada with 50 knot winds. Not a good place to be on a lee shore. But if you are prepared, the day before the front is due, pick your way thru the shoals around the island, inside the reef, stopping for lunch at this motu or that, maybe the one with the hammock under the palms, and arrive in a perfectly protected anchorage on the southeastern side. Here, breeding reefs abound. These are little patch reefs scattered here and there where the babies of the many sea creatures hide until they are big enough to protect themselves. It is a delightful experience to while away an afternoon staring at a perfectly formed starfish the size of a push pin, or a baby lobster smaller that a dime. See miniature coral trout, unbelievably small angelfish and even tiny little parrotfish. Before you know it, the northerly is over and you can return to the main anchorage, if you want. There is no hurry. No one is there. No immigration man telling you to move on, no port official telling you to pay up, no locals to ask for gasoline. It is all yours, enjoy. When was the last time no one ever bugged you? Not even a Big Guy telling you not to eat the fruit of that tree over there!

There is one guy. He used to be from New Jersey. Now he is trying to make a housing development on the island, but not trying too hard. This is Lighthouse after all. This is not a place to take the advancement of civilization too seriously. The good thing is he is connected to the internet and is glad to share. What else do you really need?

Fish. Big, shootable, eatable, fish. That's what. Outside the reef on the northwestern side of Lighthouse are a bunch of dive moorings. Belize makes the dive companies install these around the country so they don't screw up the reefs, anchoring. These companies run big, live-on-board-for-a-week dive ships. Off Lighthouse they feed the fish off the moorings and have done it for so many years that the fish not only are tame but are huge. It is impossible to describe without sounding insane. It is one of those things that you have to see for yourself, in person. The water clarity here really is astounding. Invariably, when you approach Lighthouse, the crew standing watch on the bow waves franticly, telling you to stop, turn, back up. That the water is too thin. The boat is about to run aground in 6 inches of water. They are not to be blamed; 12 feet of water does look to be 6 inches deep in Lighthouse. Another thing you just have to see for yourself.

Have I peaked your interest? Installed a desire to one day see Lighthouse for yourself? That is what this book is about, you know. A source book for day dreams. Dreams made during the day, with all your imagination working, your planning skills at their highest, all to make your dreams come true.

WEST END
ROATAN
BAY ISLANDS OF HONDURAS
WESTERN CARIBBEAN

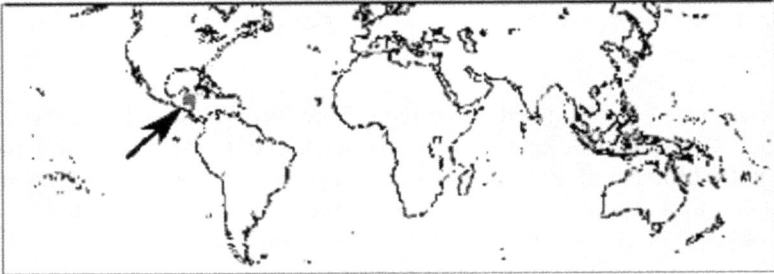

Man is fully capable of creating paradises where none existed before. The west end of Roatan is a good example of this. Before, it was a nice beach and a rather soupy, smelly lagoon. Then a developer dynamited a cut through the reef which let clean sea water into the lagoon and was deep enough, 10 feet at low tide, to allow cruising boats to enter and anchor in a protected little newly created paradise. The town of West End is what Lahaina, Maui used to be. Funky and fun, fabulous views and far, far at the end of the road where officials almost never come. Their aren't any rules except have fun and don't bug anyone enjoying themselves doing what ever comes into their little pointed heads!

The Government forces the dive companies to put in moorings around the islands and off West End for the cruisers to use. There is no charge. If you are into the town scene there are plenty of bars to go around as well as a lot of restaurants playing who can make the best cheeseburger in paradise. One is really, truly, fantastically good. Maybe second best in the Caribbean. See if you can find it!

Roatan is the center of scuba diving in this part of the world, thanks to the legendary visibility. There are so many dive shops and they are so competitive that you can still get certified for just over a 200 bucks, American. Each company has it's own housing with separate cooking facilities to keep the price down. Housing is 5 bucks a night for your own room including your own cable TV! Most Yachties talk a crew member into getting certified and then the whole crew moves in and watches TV 24 hours a day and take hot showers endlessly, while the poor student has to go out to the boat to study!

Need a funky cheap place to sail to? Try the Western Caribbean and base yourself out of West End. Checking in to the country is totally free, checking out is $3. You don't have to be rich to have the time of your lives! But you do have to smile. Wait, actually, you don't have to. But you will be smiling morning to night, anyway!   It is just what edens do to a person!

ST. HELENA
MID SOUTH ATLANTIC

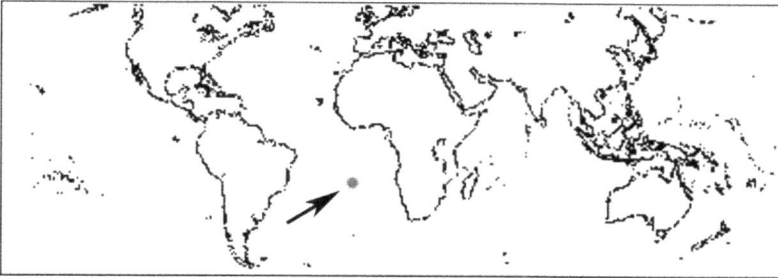

St. Helena is where they sent Napoleon to die after he escaped from Elba. It is a desolate, cliff surrounded island in the middle of the South Atlantic. At least on the outside. Once you land, climb the cliffs and get a chance to look around, it turns into a little bit of the best of England. Really, truly beautiful.   The landing is what everyone knows about. How you have to swing from your dinghy while holding on to a thick hawser, you know, like Tarzan, and land on the dock without falling in the water, or capsizing the dinghy or missing the dock and ramming, face first, into the cliffs. It would have been definitely difficult for the French to capture the island and free Napoleon what with all this swinging ashore while being shot at by the Brits.

Nowadays, the island is a sleepy little outpost of civilization and a welcome stop between Cape Town and Rio. Or at least it is if you can make the swing ashore. Don't be shy. It is difficult. But the island with all its greenness is worth it after 2 weeks at sea. Besides, like going around the Cape of Good Hope or making it past the Horn, you get to wear a gold ring in your ear if you don't get wet or smash your nose in!   British Law dictates it!

The little town of Jamestown is like walking through a history book except people are living and working in those funny looking square stone houses. The watering holes are up a few blocks so that you can see your boat from the patio. The dentist, luckily, has modern tools and the hospital is in a wood house for a change! If you want to take a tour, the bus is a roadster from years gone by. Everyone jumps in the back, convertible of course, or the jumper seats, and are escorted around. Everyone goes to Napoleon's grave even though he was dug up years ago and transplanted (if that is the right word) to Paris. It is fun to see the house where the Brits poisoned him to death by sneakily coating the house with paint laced with arsenic.

So, stop by all means. It would be a shame to pass by such a historically laden place. Besides how many people have a St. Helena stamp in their passport? And how many have a ring in both ears?

LANGKAWI
MALAYSIA
STRAITS OF MALACCA

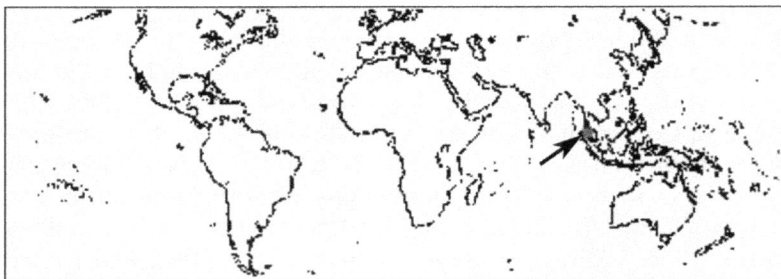

Malaysia is very nearly a fundamentalist Muslim State. It would be if the populace was a little less educated and they didn't have an underlying Asian practicality. When it comes to cruising boats and the possible evil influence they might have on the locals, the Malays came up with an elegant solution. They wanted us to spend our money and were aware that famed jet set destinations are always started by yachties talking about their newest secret paradise, but didn't want us to cause unrest by our example of unbridled freedom. So they baited a hook and threw it in the middle of an island called Langkawi. The bait is world class marinas to be had for a pittance, European beers selling for $5 a case, a minimum of paperwork and an island of unsurpassed beauty. Langkawi is so beautiful, it is difficult to describe in words lest it would sound like exaggeration.

Langkawi is an nesting island of eagles. Anytime of day many of them can be seen soaring over the peaks or zooming down to inspect your rig with that mind shattering thunder their wings make as they dive down from hundreds of feet and then applying the brakes only at the last second. Calderas of ancient volcanos are filled with fresh water and docks and staircases are built so you can anchor and then climb up and over the volcano walls to take a swim, pausing only to admire the glassy, clear, aqua blue water from the volcano rim. Langkawi is an island of caves and spelunking. Carbide lamps can be had for a song in the market to add to the sense of adventure as you delve deeper into caves filled with every different hue and shape of stalagmites and stalactites. Underground rock waterfalls abound as do once bubbling rimmed pools. Here and there, the sharp eyed will spot the six fingered handprints of the long ago inhabitants of this magical island.

Langkawi has many beautiful beaches to anchor off, fiord like inlets where you can anchor and safely survive the ultimate hurricane or tsunami. It also has a plethora of marinas. My favorite is Rebak. This marina is situated in a lagoon in the middle of a small island just off Langkawi. One day it will be another Cabo San Lucas but for now the many building lots are undeveloped save for the dirt roads that yachties use for hiking trails. There are only a few workers of the island, otherwise it is abandoned but for the many crews of visiting cruising boats. The marina was built in addition to a resort. However, no one ever comes to the resort leaving the pools, tennis courts, beach umbrellas and lounging chairs for the yachties sole use. Hourly a shore boat takes anyone who wants to go, over to the main island and to shops, grocery stores and movie theaters in the main town of Kuah. All this and floating cement docks with free power and water for $150 American a month!

Once a year, Langkawi hosts a military air show for the many third world countries in the area. Here, generals can examine planes, guns, powered parachutes, all in action and place their orders. The Soviet Migs are always the hit of the show. If you have never seen one, they are big, noisy, beautiful planes. They are only overshadowed by the smaller, quicker, faster, more maneuverable American models. For yachties, the hit of the show are always the weapons grade night vision goggles and the flying dinghies. By the way, admission is free and you can touch everything and even sit in the cockpit of the Migs!

As soon as you mention the Straits of Malacca, everyone thinks of piracy. Langkawi is filled with pirates. Not the boat stealing kind, there are none of those, the copyright stealing kind. Any movie, any software, any almost anything can be had for a buck. Malaysia maintains that it is ignoring the copyright rules until it can pull its country up by the bootstraps to first world standards and then it will start obeying them. In the meantime, what a treasure haul!

If you are in the area, or are cruising the world, stop at Langkawi. You will never regret it. It is an eden of dreams, adventure and romance! And yes, a real true shopping mecca!

FATU HIVA
MARQUESAS
FRENCH POLYNESIA
PACIFIC

Fatu Hiva is mind blowing in its beauty. As an introduction, this is what I wrote when visiting the island in 1995. It is from my book, 'Education of a Falcon'. (Available at Amazon.)

"We stopped at Fatu Hiva first. This is not really a clearance port but it is the first island we came to and the most spectacular and it was on the way, kind of. As we came into the bay, six huge black basalt spurs, 300 feet high, looking ever so much like pagan Tiki gods, loomed over us in haughty splendor. They came in pairs, one of each on either side of the entrance. We had to pass between each pair in turn. I almost felt like cowering beneath their fierce glares. At the base of the bay, a black sand beach lay with a few black rocks lurking just awash. Above the black on black of the beach, green coconut palms feathered the valley. Above the palms, in the distance, the white of a waterfall broke the black mountains into

two halves. Below the palms, the colorfully dressed Marquesans played soccer, darting this way and that like so many birds. Not many first impressions are as fabulous as this. No wonder so many of Bligh's men mutinied!"

These days the island is equally as beautiful. There are no stores, no shops, nothing that operates on money. This is a barter society. If you intend to barter for carvings or tattoos or veggies, bring a wide variety of goods. There is no telling what the boats before you have saturated the market with! Be sure to visit at least one of the waterfalls. There are many.

This island is where Thor Heyerdahl of Kon Tiki fame came with his new bride to live at peace in nature. It worked alright for a few months but by the end of a year, they and the locals were glad to split company. Enjoy the island, barter happily away, swim in the waterfall, but don't ever ask how much land costs or what property might be for sale! This is a very inbred society who enjoy outsiders as long as they remain outsiders. Sometimes the most beautiful places have the most troubled people. But that doesn't make the island less of a paradise. Even Adam and Eve couldn't spend their whole lives in Eden. They tried to buy into the hierocracy by eating of the forbidden fruit and got thrown out for disobeying the rules. A lot of the best places have unwritten rules. But they are great places to visit and no one expects temporary visitors to know all the rules and traditions! Enjoy your eden maybe even build a grass shack on the beach, but if anyone asks, you are leaving very soon!

VAVA'U

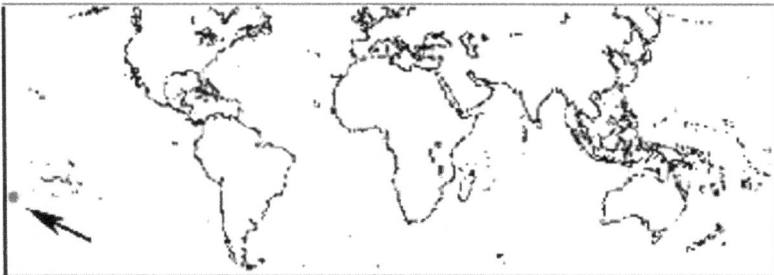

TONGA
PACIFIC OCEAN

Tonga is one of the few countries that were never conquered by invading civilizations, mostly because they ate any strangers who happened to come around for the most of their history. Afterwards, when they were 'civilized' a series of very able kings managed to work one European power against the other, aided by the fact that Tonga didn't have anything that civilization wanted, anyway. It is different now. Our civilizations have changed. Everyone wants what Tonga has now, but the king still excels at working one group of invading tourist against the other. Flights are canceled and cruise ships are forbidden entry at the whim of the king. The only sure way to visit Tonga is on your own boat. And you do, really, want to visit! Really!

The best part of Tonga is the northern section, Vava'u. Years ago the Moorings Charter Group established a base there and lacking any decent chart, drew their own. It is still in use today by visiting yachts. Tongan islands have very long, all most unpronounceable names. On the Moorings chart, they labeled the 30 most fantastic anchorages by numbers. It wasn't long before everyone was referring to Nukalofalofaneehou by the number 24, even the locals! Those first 30 (there are more now) anchorages are some of the most beautiful in the world. In each, a local family puts on a feast once a week for the boats anchored off their island. They are real local feasts consisting of what the family caught that day: lobsters and pig, many kinds of fish, abundance of local fruit and veggies, served on banana leaves, eaten with fingers, washed down with local hooch. The little kids dance, the teenage beauties serve the food, the older ladies cook, the men pour the booze. Each feast is different, but almost all end with the kids going to bed and the yachties joining the locals dancing half naked around a roaring bonfire. Vava'u is really great. It isn't something that is easy to describe. Don't yell at me! Go there and then see if you can do better!

The Tongans are very industrious and you can buy many exquisite carvings, a variety of tapa cloth art work, go for horse back rides, swim in holy caves almost filled with water. If you are there when the King makes his yearly visit, be prepared for a massive feast that defies belief. No wonder no one ever conquered the Tongans. They believe in carrying everything to extremes! Especially eating and dancing!

Normally, if you are westbound across the trades from Tahiti, you have to decide whether to visit Tonga or the Samoas before carrying on to Fiji. Both are great. American Samoa your last chance, for a long time, to buy American products, Tonga for the parties of a lifetime. I say do both. Yes, you will be hard on the wind one way or the other, but that it is only for a couple hundred miles. And by this time, after so many sea miles, you will have turned into a true bluewater passage maker.

A warning. Tongan families turn the first child into a caretaker/babysitter, even if the first is a male. So if you are dancing with the locals, and if one of the larger girls seems very interested in you, be careful! He/she may not be what you are quite expecting!

But whatever you do, don't miss Vava'u! It is cruising at its finest and is a wonderful eden!

ACAPULCO
MEXICO
PACIFIC OCEAN

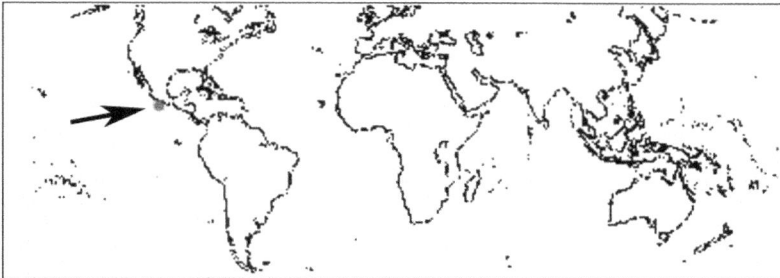

Acapulco is a vibrant, exciting city. I like everything about it, the markets, the people, being surrounded at night by a circle of light while anchored, I even like watching the cliff divers while trying to avoid being pick pocketed! It is a great city! Most people don't like it. Most people hate Acapulco. They hate it because the anchorage is too deep, is too expensive, is too crowded, is too out of the way and they feel they are being cheated. Even if they do like the place they don't stay long. The marinas are only for the rich and famous and the mooring field isn't far behind. If you don't mind shortening the life of your windless, you can anchor in 70 feet and swing within inches of your neighbors. Not for me. There are other anchorages in the bay. You can anchor at islands and at other beaches with endless jet skis. That's not for me either. They are too far away from the city that we came to see. There is a solution. A great solution. A perfect beach, 18 foot deep anchorage, secure dinghy area and no jet skis. It only has one drawback. This anchorage is deep in the bay just to the north of the navy base there. The base is a gorgeous anchorage but they don't seem to enjoy our company for some incomprehensible reason. However, just to the north, just over the line, they don't care. Jet skis are not welcome within 100 meters of the base line, something to do with potential terrorists. The border is well guarded with sailors with sub-machine guns and beady eyes. Don't scowl at them. They are going to guard our dinghy! There is a rope laid down the border to let tourists know when the shooting starts. The guards don't mind us tying the dinghy off on this line while pulled up the beach. Believe me no one is going to mess with it with those guys staring out of dead pan eyes. No one even sunbathes within 100 feet of the line. The main road runs just a block inside the beach, across the road is the largest Wal-mart you have ever seen, down the street are supermarkets and a short bus ride away is the city market. You do want to go to this market! It is the one that all other markets in the world are compared to! Anchored here you are in the middle of the vibrant city you came to see. True if you came for the famed restaurants and the cliff divers, it is a long way away. But there are unfamed wonderfully creative restaurants just off the city center and we have all seen the cliff divers endless times on the Wild World of Sports without the hassle of pickpockets.

The snake in this eden is the wind switches from off shore during the day, which keeps your bow into the ever present southwesterly swell, to parallel to the shore putting you sideways to the swell during the night. Not fun but not a problem. On the otherside of the navy base is a small bay that is loaded with jet skis and anchored boats during the day. During the night they all go home leaving this swell free bay all for us. It is 30 to 40 feet to anchor here but there is usually a mooring or two you can pick up for free. No, we can't stay here during the day as well as the land goes straight up and you have to hike inland and hundreds of feet up to get to the first bus line. But not a problem. In the morning the swell is down, the wind switches to on shore and we re-anchor back by our own beady eyed guard!

So many people bypass Acapulco, needlessly. It is one of the stars of the Pacific side of Mexico. A city of legend, of beauty, of memories and of a great anchorage. Or rather a set of great anchorages! Is Acapulco a real eden? I remember, during the cut flower season, walking down 4 city blocks of flowers in the market, surrounded by the scent of millions of flowers.

I remember one holiday, anchored in the bay while fireworks burst forth from 360° along the cliffs of the circular bay. I remember seeing a young boy leaping from the cliffs to his certain death on the exposed rocks far below. Of his innocent body falling head first to be torn apart, mangled and destroyed. Tears came to my eyes as a wave suddenly, miraculously, surged in at the last second to cover the sharp, black rocks and save him. It was enough to convert the heathen to Christianity. I remember a pickpocket running away from his victim only to stop and help an old lady cross the street and away from a racing bus. I remember a vibrant city that still sends echos of longing through my soul. What is an eden anyway? A place you miss so much that you spend your life hoping to go back one day?

MAJURO
MARSHALL ISLANDS
MICRONESIA
WESTERN PACIFIC

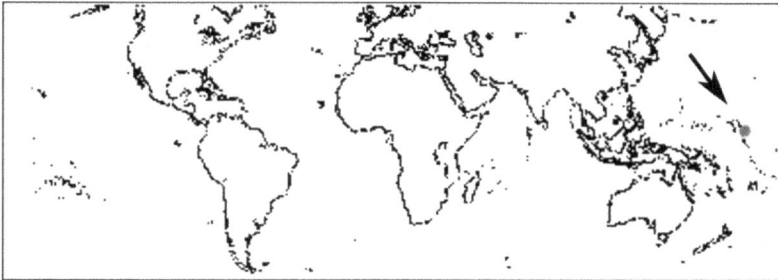

In the old days, following WWII, most of the islands conquered by the Japanese in the Pacific were lumped into a group labeled the 'Trust Territory.' This included the Marshalls, the Carolines (including Palau and Yap) and the Marianas. In 1986 the Trust was dissolved and new countries were formed including the Marshalls of which Majuro is the capitol. It is a country of atolls the most famous of which are Bikini (where the first H bomb was exploded) and Kwajalein, even today a missile testing site. They are beautiful islands well worth a visit especially Majuro. Almost all of the people live on the eastern most of the islands that are connected by bridges. You have to make your own fun in Majuro, but that isn't hard to do.

The road connecting the islands is half of a mile long and is serviced by a fleet of taxis. What, you say? Taxis to go a half a mile? Yes, it costs a quarter to go from one end of the road to the other. They are share taxis so they pick up more people as they drive along and the locals use the taxis as a vehicle for gossip. But you have to gossip very fast before you get to the other end! The Majuroans (if that is a word) don't make leis like in Hawaii. Instead they make ornate flower head bands out of many different types of flowers. Not only are they works of art, but they will last for a week! So there you are, crowded into a taxi, because it is only a quarter, with everyone talking at the same time and the entire car is filled with the indescribable aroma of hundreds of tropical flowers and you are stuck in the middle and can't get out, but it is ok as the road is only half a mile so it doesn't matter how slow the taxi goes so that everyone can wave at their friends as it will all be over in just a few minutes! You do your business at the end of the island and then, for some strange reason, take another taxi back again! At least it isn't boring!

There are a lot of aid workers on Majuro from many different countries. They are supplied with their own car (why?) so they can't take the taxis to relieve boredom. Instead they become seriously determined wild party people. It is a unique experience to be sitting in a house, getting seriously drunk, with everyone talking in different languages all at once and then going out to swim in the lagoon. It is a good thing that the sharks have all been fished out or they would be getting very fat!

It is hard to say what is so cool about Majuro. I think it is that everyone is out to have a good time any which way they can! Does that sound good to you? Is that paradise to you? They use American dollars, it is regular postage to mail to the USA, and the groceries are about the same price as Hawaii, and it is quasi legal to work there. So what exactly is keeping you away? Inertia?

ISLA MOZAMBIQUE
MOZAMBIQUE
INDIAN OCEAN

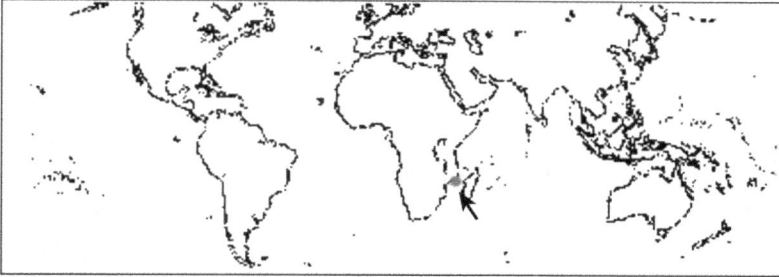

In 1497 Vasco de Gama was the first to round the Cape of Good Hope and head into the Indian Ocean. He traveled on to India where he established the city of Goa. Along the way he discovered the Island of Mozambique and built a fort there. The island became the most secure port that Portugal possessed in the Indian ocean, and remained that way until Mozambique gained its independence.

Today, Isla Mozambique has fallen on hard times militarily but is booming in the tourist and the sunken treasure trade. There are over 600 identified wrecks within 2 miles of the island and 14 of those sank in the 1500's. They are all protected, of course, but just walking around the island is enough to educate you beyond belief. The roads are made of half crushed dishes from China. I am not joking. Who needs to go to a museum when you can just pick up half a plate on the street. Late at night, in that dark alley your mother told you about, shady characters sell artifacts from the sunken ships. I bought a carved pewter and bronze mug that belongs in the Smithsonian for $2! Children in the middle of the day sell necklaces of the original trade beads used by explorers in the 14th century to buy information and porters! The entire island is a museum.

Divers from around the world come to Isla Mozambique to help with the mapping and exploration of the many wrecks. While we were there they brought up what they were sure was a Phoenician ship from the 13th century that must have come down from the Red Sea. After they finished mapping and recording their finds on the ship, they sink it back in the same place as they found it in the belief that if the sea could preserve it for so many centuries, it would continue to preserve it for many more to come. What other secrets does such a natural fort as Isla Mozambique hold?

The Fort on the only hill on the island is still in good shape, or at least in as good a shape as it ever was. It is made with red ballast stones which might not be state of the art now but was quite effective in the 1500's when the ultimate warship was a caravel armed with small breech loaders which tended to explode randomly killing their crew. Weeds grow in the parade ground, the cannon have been shipped off to Europe but the walls still stand proud and a few of the houses still have their roofs.

Mozambique is blessed and cursed by the southbound Agulhas Current. This is a strong current which can reach 8 knots in places. Great if you are heading south with a north wind, not so great in the wind is from the south and you have wind against tide conditions. If this happens to you, duck in somewhere. In fact, duck in to Isla Mozambique. You will have an experience you will never forget!

We busted a bearing in our engine's fresh water pump coming down from Mayotte. There were no replacements to be had in Isla Mozambique but I traveled into one of the larger towns inland on a hope and a prayer. Not a bearing could be found. However a machine shop made the bearings and the race by hand. And it worked, perfectly! Edens are where miracles occur daily, aren't they? Go to Isla Mozambique and see if it won't perform a miracle for you!

DIRECTION ISLAND
COCOS KEELING
INDIAN OCEAN

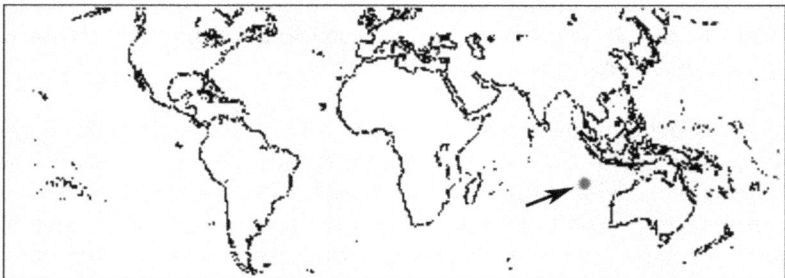

Cocos Keeling atoll was very famous once. It was discovered late in the history of the world in 1609 but not settled until 1826 by an Englishman named Alexander Hare who peopled his island with just himself and a harem of 26 of the sexiest Malay women he could find. Newspapers were full of the story in those days and Hare became the idol of a generation of explorers. Because of all the publicity, he didn't have his islands to himself very long. Just the next year he was invaded by the Clunies-Ross family who brought along 26 Malay men! Hare didn't put up much of a fight, but then he was probably very tired! The island stayed in the news for a few years until Charles Darwin visited looking for new species before traveling to the Galapagos Islands and the history books. Then the atoll slowly slid into obscurity. It belongs to Australia these days which bought it from the Clunies-Ross Family in 1978. Hare died an early death alone and abandoned by his harem. Maybe he should have only brought 7 women? One for each day of the week?

Way back then, people lived on only a couple of the islands or motus, as islands on outer reefs are called. Direction Island, the first one on the east as you enter the pass has never been occupied as there is little water. Too bad as it is one of the most beautiful islands in the world. The beach, as white as can be, stretches out in an arc with over hanging coconut palms. Beach lovers will enjoy it but the amazing part is a small pass on the south of Direction Island. Not only is the pass filled with fish and sharks, plants and corals of the most beautiful kind, but the water always flows inward. If you leave your boat, swim the short 100 feet to shore, walk over to small pass and jump in with your mask and fins, the current will carry you through all the incredible sea life, empty you back into the lagoon and flush you right back to the side of your boat. Directly right back to your boat! Everyone then swims back to the beach and repeats the experience hour after hour, it is so cool!

Cocos Keeling is one of the last of the really great duty free ports. The stores are on West Island. A ferry will take you there from Direction Island and return you to your boat with all your cases of liquid refreshment that you will need in Chagos!

There is no doubt that Cocos Keeling is an Eden. There are few places more beautiful in the world and it is one of those rare places of power where you are refreshed, restored and your body healed as you lay on the sands under the overhanging palms. Anywhere on the horseshoe beach works and when you feel like a child again, go float down the pass and out to your boat over and over again until you laugh in joy!

SAN BLAS ISLANDS
PANAMA
CARIBBEAN SEA

The people of the San Blas Islands, the Kunas, are the second smallest people on earth beat out only by the pygmies of Darkest Africa. Never the less, they share with the Tongans the right to say they have never been conquered by any foreign power. While the Tongans are some of the largest and toughest people on earth and can take on anybody, the San Blas Indians are really small and they only survived by running away and hiding. It was easy to do. They live on a series of 365 islands off the coast of Panama. They have farms on a thin strip of land on the mainland. There are lots of hiding spots. As soon as the would be conquerors started feasting to celebrate their effortless victory over the abandoned islands, the Kunas would appear seemingly out of nowhere and kill the would be warriors, then go into hiding again. After a while, conqueror nations dried up and the Kunas were left in peace.

Today they are still in peace. The women sew fantastic reverse appliqué designs to be put on shirts or bags for cash money. The men still go out fishing in their sail driven log canoes in the afternoon and go farming in the mornings. It is the living ideal of the Jeffersonian belief of a perfect civilization of primary producers. Much like the Amish, they turn their backs on modern advances and are interested instead in interpersonal relationships. It is a matriarchal society with power and money residing with the wife's mother's husband. The women display their wealth with large gold rings worn through the septum of the nose. The Kunas consider the little motus residing at the edge of the reefs as fairly worthless. Good for coconuts and as a place to go fishing once or twice a month. All the action is on the islands close to the mainland. They leave these absolutely beautiful islands to the yachties. Imagine if you will, a little island the size of a couple tennis courts, populated with coconut palms, with a washing well and a drinking well on opposite ends of the island which is surrounded with the whitest, softest sand beach you have ever seen or felt. And you are alone anchored off this island, unless you are kind and tell your buddies where your island is. The Kunas don't care as long as you don't harvest too many of the coconuts.

After rigging your hammock and lounging around for a few days, you might want to jump in the sea with your little pole spear. Look under a couple of rocks. See all the little lobsters? They aren't lobsters. They are an unreported species. Don't tell any biologists! They are black in color with small white polka dots and are unbelievably delicious, far better than a Maine lobster.

So there you are living in eden with all you need from civilization. What else do you require? Look over there on the horizon. It is a Kuna canoe heading towards you. Don't freak out. This is the San Blas. If any pirates ever came the Kunas would take care of them late at night. Instead of freaking out, get your one dollar bills together. The canoe comes alongside and he is selling everything under the sun, from frozen chicken, fruit, eggs, beer and bread. If you want something else he will have it for you next week! A couple days later, another canoe comes around that last point of the island. This one is selling diesel. Everything you might need is brought to you. There is no need to leave, ever. There is no place on earth as close to the original Eden as the outer San Blas Islands.

Boats coming from the Pacific and the relative calms of the lee of Central America, have their eyes opened by the trades blowing 20 to 25 day and night, nonstop, outside the harbor walls of Colon. You have to reef down and get used to tacking and making just a few knots. You have to make some windward distance to the east so that when you turn north, you will be clear of a reef strewn Central American lee shore. One of the best ways to do this is to beat out to the San Blas and spend some time recovering. It doesn't matter if it is a few weeks or the rest of your life, the islands are worth it. If your visa is up, sail down the entire San Blas chain and clear into Columbia and then return to the San Blas with a brand new visa. What could be easier. The worse part of finding an eden is leaving it. But then, why leave?

LORD HOWE
AUSTRALIA
TASMAN SEA

The Tasman is perhaps the consistently roughest piece of water on the planet. There is no reason to go anywhere near there. Yes, if you want to go to Sydney from New Zealand or from Fiji, it seems logical and shorter to pass right through the middle of the Tasman. But check out the cruising guides. They add 3 times the mileage on their routes, just to keep you out of the Tasman. However, if you are an ornery kind of person or don't believe in cruising guides, there is a reason to visit the middle of the Tasman, a little Island called Lord Howe. It is a tall volcanic island surrounded by coral reefs. There is a tiny pass on the southwestern side. Normally you call ahead on the VHF and the Port Captain will guide you via VHF through the reefs from the cliffs far above. Once inside you are in a wonderland. Sweet smelling pine trees populate the island interspersed with rare plants and bird life unique to the island. They are protected by national parks which cover 70% of the island. The island's mountains are extremely sheer, so much so that on an isolated rock just south and east of the main island, sunlight can be seen not thru a hole but right through the thin, living rock.

We went through a the eye of a Cat 5 hurricane on Lord Howe. Any time an island protects you from the ravages of a 5, the memory of the place is carried, unmarred by time, in a special locker in your heart to be pulled out when you wake up in the middle of the night and can't sleep because of heavy trades blowing in your rig. But don't take my word for it. Go and look for yourself. It is one of those special places that will change you forever, just by breathing the air, swimming in the lagoon and gazing at the sun through the rock of the mountain itself!

LARNACA
CYPRUS
MEDITERRANEAN

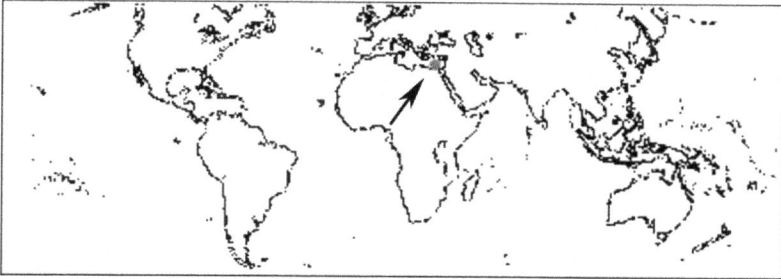

After the ravages of beating up the Red Sea and avoiding the pirates in the Gulf of Aden, a passage making sailor is ready for some rest and relaxation. Egypt is a great place but there is always an undercurrent of unrest. Israel is ok but it is just too damn expensive. But luckily, there is a wonderful island plopped right in the middle of the Eastern Med just waiting for us.

Cyprus is a divided island, half Turkish and half Greek. These two countries have hated each other since Paris stole Helen. You would think time would heal all wounds, wouldn't you? Not in this case. However, instead of fighting and rattling sabers, the two halves of Cyprus compete with each other seeing who can be the most hospitable to tourists. For sailors, the best and friendliest port is Larnaca, which is on the southern Greek side. This is a classic Med town, except the marina is reasonable, the market is full of artichokes and the sailors have grips of iron, the kind of grip you only get from short tacking up a thousand miles of the Red Sea.

Every night the sailors, still celebrating getting past the pirates and surviving the sand storms, gather in a local bistro and eat $1 kebabs. Afterwards, it is time to go to the patisserie where the pastries and baklava are delicious and only a quarter a piece. Life is good in Larnaca. Draw a big red circle around it on your planning chart. It is a great introduction to the Med or for those heading down the Big Red, a final glorious goodbye.

PROVIDENCE TOWN
CAPE COD
MASSACHUSETTS
ATLANTIC OCEAN

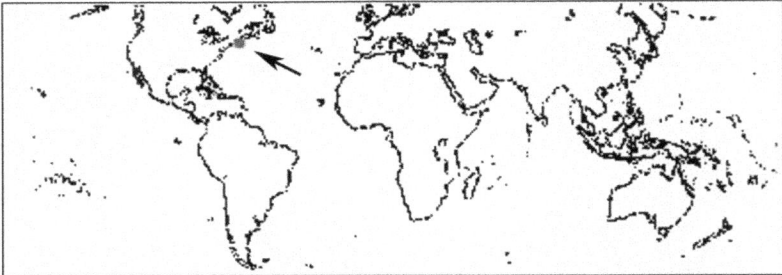

Providence Town is a gay town. Yes, it is happy and carefree, but it is also inhabited by an overwhelming population of homosexuals and lesbians. The rest of the world seems to fear these people calling them deviants or worse. They should visit Providence Town. It is a town of happiness, of joy, of hospitality and of the sea. The harbor is filled with moorings and marinas but there is room to anchor here and there. Once ashore, the town shows its true colors. Artwork is everywhere. Some houses look like something out of the Lord of the Rings, with round doors and twisted sidewalks. Artists weld up wind chimes of every different description. Only slightly less inventive, locals organize dog shows with each dog dressed as wildly as possible displaying the owner's sexual preferences.

When you are finished exploring the dark side, travel along the hundreds of miles of abandoned beaches. They are wild and wind swept, much like they must have been when the pilgrims landed just north of here, and are still unchanged after all these centuries. Today the only sign of man might be a splintered hatch off of a boat or a half sunken life ring which raises more questions than answers. The bay is a summer retreat for countless whales, come down from the cold arctic to bear young and make love. There are so many that at times you find yourself weaving your boat thru them rather than pointing at a distant horizon.

The library in Providence Town is first class. Not only does it have lightning quick free internet service but it has countless shows displaying relics of ancient ships and nautical history. The middle of the building is open to the ceiling, some five stories up to make room for the tall masts belonging to ships on display.

If ever you are making the run up to Maine for the summer, don't bypass Providence Town, it is just past the Cape Cod Canal and a little south and east of Boston. It is a great and interesting port of call and a true paradise for some! Now, now, don't be judgmental. To earn a place in Eden, one has to learn never to qualify others by how they fit in with your preferences!

WATER ISLAND
ST. THOMAS
US VIRGIN ISLANDS
CARIBBEAN SEA

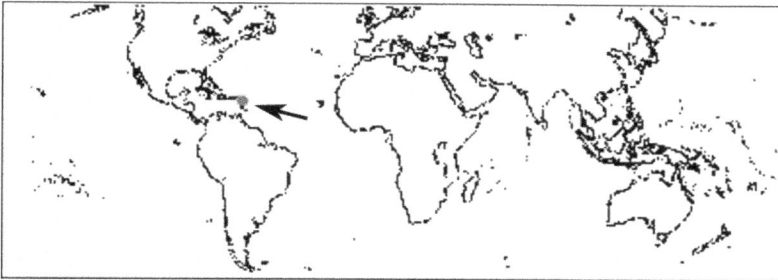

Water Island lies just south and west of Charlotte Amalie, capital and main seaport of the American Virgins. The Department of the Interior in D.C. retained control of the island for years after the Virgins' gained a degree of self government. People were allowed to build houses on the island and claim ownership if they improved the property under the Homestead Act. Few people did this however. Water Island remained a little known paradise. And a paradise it is to this day.

Years ago, pirates used the island as a source of water and as a lookout point for passing Spanish treasure laden galleons. They anchored off the same beach as you will. (In pirates days, the island was Skull Island and the beach was Bloody Sands). Now the beach is called Honeymoon Cove and a more perfect spot for a bit of romance would be hard to find. The sand is pure white studded with coconut trees. Play in the gentle surf line when you are there. Run your fingers through the sand. Many a sailor has found pirate loot in much the same way. Our dog, Ilia, dug up a hundred dollar bill. So, old or new, the booty is there.

The sand is fine grained and lovely, just right for questing fingers, give it a try!

Once a week, the locals spread sewn together bed sheets between two palm trees and show movies free to whoever shows up. Just before the movie, the cooks from the island's restaurants bring down their wares for sale on the beach, including the absolutely best cheeseburger in paradise bar none. I know many will insist they know a place with a better burger, but in the interest of scientific investigation, give this one a try.

The Island is connected to the 'mainland' of St. Thomas by a passenger ferry which occasionally also carries a postman who drops off the mail in covered boxes by the pier. So after you watch the sunrise, drink your coffee and take the first (and most healthy) rays of the sun on your naked body, jump in your unregistered car or electric golf cart and drive down to pick up your mail. There was no government on Water Island for close to 50 years. It was nominally under the control of the US Government but they didn't care what people did. Eventually they gave the island to St Thomas and the local governor took charge. He took one look and said, "What a Paradise!" and left it more or less alone after he bought a house on top of a hill. The Homestead Act no longer applied once the island was handed over but there are many half ruined houses on the island that need fixing up. I really doubt anyone would be concerned if you moved in. The island is mountainous so every house has an outstanding view. What exactly are you waiting for?

As always the people make the difference. Whether you love an island or not depends on how the locals agree with your lifestyle. If you are a bit wild and carefree, if you like to dabble in the arts, if you like to turn your yard into a wonderland of flowers, this might be your island.

You can take it in stages. Many property owners fly off to the States for months at a time and need dependable people to water the plants and feed the dogs. On an island like this, it is surprising how easy it is to meet strangers and to become bosom buddies in a few hours. Imagine living on top of a mountain, the Caribbean laid below your feet, your boat anchored securely in Honeymoon Bay far below and breakfast is hanging from the myriad of fruit trees surrounding your house. It must have been like this in the original Eden.

Today there is no question that Water Island is a beautiful Eden. One you should definitely add to you list of cruising destinations! It may not change you when you breathe the air, but not to worry, you will be having too much fun and your life will be filled with too much pleasure to notice.

SAFI

MOROCCO

ATLANTIC OCEAN

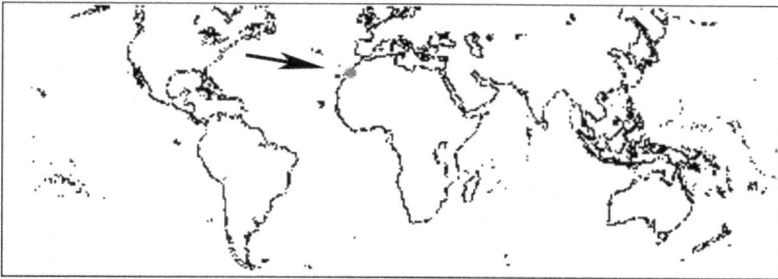

There aren't many old Arab towns left. It is a shame, it is. They were so unique, so wild, so different. These days one city looks much like another and if you couldn't read, you couldn't even tell what continent you are on. But not if it is Safi. This city is still true to it's old self.

The seawalls of the port are huge to protect the harbor against the ravages of the Atlantic Storms common hereabouts. That is probably why you are here. No one has ever heard of Safi. Why would you go there intentionally? It is off the beaten track, the way the best edens are. As you approach, notice that the same fishing smacks seem to be going in and out of the port over and over again. Very strange. The port captain has you tie up with the other sailboats, mostly French as they speak French in Morocco. They are nice enough docks, especially for the price, gratis. The same boats are still going back and forth. Weird. There must be another fishing harbor around the corner of the breakwater. But why back and forth?

The town is delightful. As always, in older Arab towns the streets are twisty, constantly turning this way and that. The devil, it seems, likes to travel in straight lines. Safi is an older town. It was founded by the Carthaginians, who were replaced in turn by the Romans, Jews, Goths and finally the Muslims who used it as a ribat (a fortress of the holy war). I guess the twisty streets were good against an invading army, too! The central market is great. Right there in front of your eyes, inhabitants are practicing their trade. Candle makers are tapering many shapes and sizes of candles, leather makers are finishing off their hides, farmers display a dizzying array of produce and potters have stores loaded with the pottery that Safi is famed for in the Muslim world.

Finally your wanderings carry you to the south side of town and a huge harbor opens up, a harbor occupied by thousands of fishing smacks. The same boats weren't going in and out, they were different boats of the same color scheme!

So what is so eden like about Safi? It is hard to say. Some places in the world call out to you. Call out to some resonating sounding board in your soul. Whether it is the merchants selling myrrh, frankincense and dragon's blood. (I know you are going to ask! Dragon's Blood is obtained from the fruit of palms [Daemonorops] and traditionally used in Europe as an ingredient in the varnish to paint violins. In Mexico, it is used as a medicine to heal wounds that refuse to close, from whence it got its name.) Or if the twisty streets remind you of childhood where direction finding consisted of the unraveling of streets that all seemed to be too complicated, then that is part of eden, too.

While following the twisting streets be prepared to happen on people of legend. Sword swallowers, fire eaters and fortune tellers dwell in little coves along the dusty byways. Gaze into their eyes and feel what life on earth once was not so many years ago. Is their romance and adventure in history? You betcha! How many vacations can you take lying on a beach or skiing on a slope? Try something different.

Is Safi a true Eden? Of all the paradises I have listed within, Safi was the one I questioned if it should be included the most. All I can tell you is, go there. Breathe the air, eat the fruit, walk the streets. Something within you might reverberate with some forgotten echo. Something might awaken in your soul making you a more complex and interesting person. Give Safi a try, after all, not all paradises are tropical or sand floored!

THE TURNING BASIN
WASHINGTON, D.C.
POTOMAC RIVER

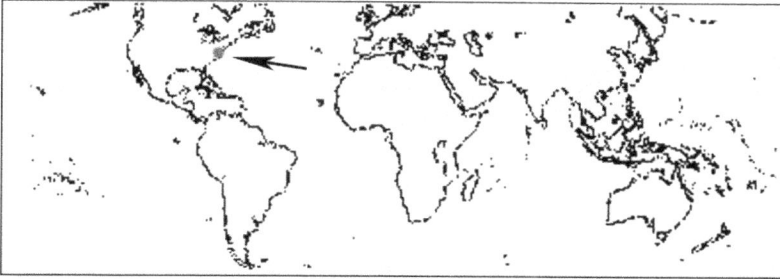

Paradises have a hard time existing in major cities, especially ones where so many self-serving people work. But miracles happen. In this case, a whole series of miracles! The first being that there is a free anchorage within 2 football fields of the Washington Monument, not only free, but perfectly protected! This in one of the most aggressive cities in the world!

The second miracle is a yacht club that lets us cut-offs wearing, backpack toting, baseball cap covered, bearded and sandaled yachties share it's premises with America's senators and representatives, charging only $5 a day for the run of the club! The third miracle is caused by the fact that yachties almost always travel up the Potomac in summer when the temperature soars into the high 90's.

This miracle is the Smithsonian Institute that lies 4 blocks from the turning basin, is open late and has the coldest air conditioning in Washington. If you haven't been recently, the Smithsonian has developed far beyond the best museum in the world. It takes weeks to get through it all, the displays have been changed into hands on, interactive experiences and there are tunnels connecting all the buildings so there is no need to go out into the heat. As if in jealousy, other government agencies have started to compete. The Postal Service has a great museum honoring the pony express where Indians 'fire' arrows at you as you 'carry' the mail through woods and on to the next exhibit.

Is Washington D. C. an eden? Maybe not, but it is a miracle and that is the next best thing. Maybe even better!

BORA BORA
FRENCH POLYNESIA
PACIFIC OCEAN

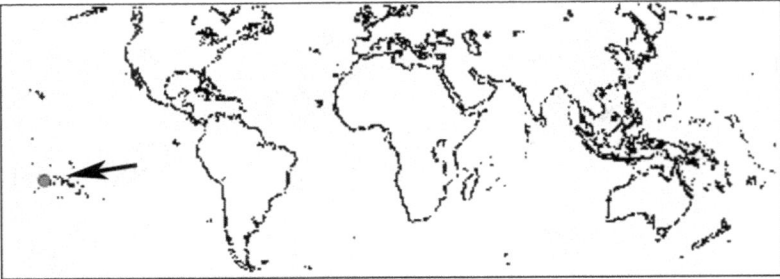

Bora Bora is a true paradise. Everyone who has ever been there agrees. No one disagrees. If you asked everyone who has never been there to name the most romantic, beautiful eden in the world, they would vote for Bora Bora overwhelmingly. Ask people who have been there and they will tell you that there is only one Bora Bora. The truth is; it is even better than they could ever dream! It is the complete package.

True, Bora Bora lacks the fantastic simplicity of an Ant or a Chagos, but it makes up for it with 5 star French restaurants. True, the hotels slightly mar the shoreline, but for that kind of food, who cares about a few buildings here and there. Besides they are disguised with coconut trees and a wide variety of flowers.

The best thing for me about Bora Bora is on the east side of the island, on the southeast side of the channel, there is a 70 foot spot where giant, 20' across, manta rays soar across the incoming tide acting like fighter pilots in a dog fight. Those who are brave and with scuba gear and a wet suit can grab hold of a wing and have the experience of a life time. The mantas don't seem to care. You do have to find room amongst the myriad of 5 foot remoras. Or be like Karen and just grab hold of the remora instead. Even if you just snorkel around to enjoy the show, it will be an experience that you will never forget. The wet suit is to protect your tummy and chest from the shark like skin of the mantas. Don't leave home without it!

Papeete, on Tahiti, hosts Bastille Day where all the athletes from the outer islands come to compete on July 14th . Except the locals call it

"Liberation from the French Day"! It is cool and all, but far better is Bora Bora's liberation day which takes place on July 28th. Instead of running around trying to see everything in Papeete, relax on Bora Bora where all the events are in the same open square. You just have to go to see the Tamari dancers. If you ever went to Hawaii and saw the Tahitian dancers, you ain't seen nothing yet till you see Bora Borans on their own turf. Wow!

The core of Liberation Day is the outrigger canoe race featuring teams from all over the world. Everyone competes equally, but in reality it has turned into a grudge race between teams from Tahiti, Hawaii and Bora Bora. The race starts at Point Venus (the same place Captain Cook sailed half way around the world to observe the Transit of Venus against the face of the Sun. This was important back then as it established, finally, the circumference of the earth and the distance between the Earth and the Sun.) Point Venus is a far better anchorage than Papeete.

You want to be at the start of the race as you can go ashore and see and touch all the canoes lined up on the beach and see all the paddlers. Guys, if you thought you were in shape, think again. Girls, you can touch the men instead of the canoe, if you present a lei first! Anyway, if the year you are there, Bora Bora wins, you have to be in Bora Bora on July 28th. It will be the biggest, wildest party you have ever seen! No one can teach the Bora Borans anything about parties. Let me give you a clue. The girls don't wear those green panties under the grass skirts when their men win the canoe race!

You will love Bora Bora. Everyone does. I bet you can't wait to get there! If there is just only one Bora Bora, why don't we just call it Bora?

BRISBANE
QUEENSLAND
AUSTRALIA

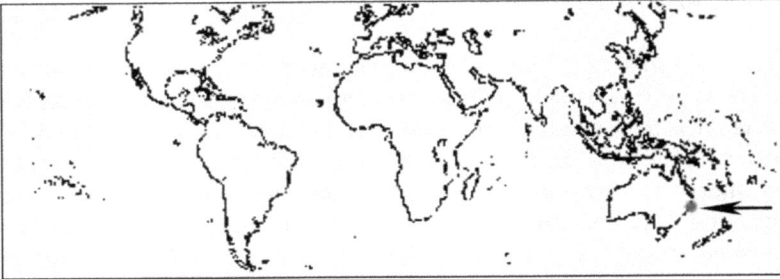

Brisbane is a great Australian city. It didn't used to be. It started as a penal colony in 1824 then a hundred years later, turned into a cow town full of beer drinking, rowdy cowboys with a wild river that flooded with a huge 15 foot wall of water every time it rained. Not any more. They dammed up the river, kept the cowboys on the outskirts and built one of the most fantastic and accessible botanical gardens in the world. And just to do everything right they put in moorings and a dinghy dock right in the middle of the gardens.

Imagine waking in the morning to the scent of hundreds of exotic flowers and the laughing cry of the famed kookaburra. Imagine walking to the grocery or marine store along paved trails, cooled by some of the most beautiful trees and plants on Earth. For Free! To keep bar-be-que mad Australians from setting the whole thing on fire, they built propane fired pits, surrounded with picnic tables, on grass hills overlooking the river here and there thru the Garden. Cost? 25 cents for an hour of propane! Just in case you get tired of the botanical garden, the dinghy dock is right next to a passenger ferry dock, which for $5 a week will take you up and down the river, stopping at many malls each with their own docks. Who needs to tote groceries?

On the opposite side of the garden, across the river, is the play area of Brisbane. Here famed musicians from around the world come to play for your enjoyment. Your Free Enjoyment! Play areas for the kids abound. Tennis, handball and basketball courts are free. Along the river bank are beautiful artificial sand beaches just in case all this fun is too much for you and you just have to take a break and catch a few rays or just need to adore the sight of some female flesh!

Want some culture? Museums? Art? Movies? Plays? Opera? The symphony? Brisbane is the capitol of Queensland, and is a major player among the world's great cities. So you have just crossed the Pacific, stopped at native villages and abandoned islands, stood who knows how many night watches, fought squall after squall, and somehow made it through with boat and marriage intact. Don't you think you could use a little pampering? Haven't you earned it?

Soon enough you will be banging up the Great Barrier Reef. There aren't that many places with quality rest and relaxation, right next to the boat. Get out your little atlas. Put a big red circle around Brisbane. You won't regret it! As a Eden for the rich and famous, only the Left Bank can compete. For us yachties who put every spare cent we have into the boat, Eden and free are synonyms!

SABA
NETHERLANDS ANTILLES
CARIBBEAN SEA

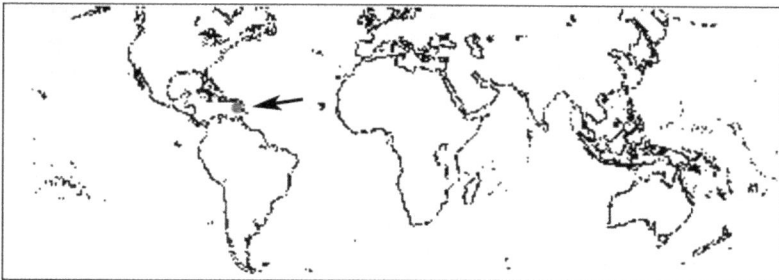

Not many people visit Saba. There is not a good port. The roadstead could kindly be described as marginal. There are no beaches. The two eateries are more snack bars than restaurants. The people are insular and distant. How could it possibly be described as an eden? It is beyond belief. It is an eden, though. One of the most remarkable in the world.

Saba is the peak of an ancient extinct volcano. The main town, up a long road from the landing, is called Bottom as it is situated in the caldera of the volcano's crater. The highest point, 2910', is Mt. Misery. It is the climbing of this peak that qualifies Saba as an eden. First a warning, politicians are trying to change the name of Mt. Misery to Mt. Scenery. Don't be fooled. It is a long hard slog, especially for over fed sailors. At the bottom of the mountain, in Bottom, many signs relate the beauty you will discover at the top of the mountain. The many

Caribbean Islands you will see in all their glory. The snapshots you will use to entertain your friends and family. It won't happen. The top of Mt. Misery lives eternally in clouds of the densest kind. But not to worry. The view, or rather non-view, is not what qualifies Saba as an eden either.

It will be a struggle to make it to the top. Don't be a martyr. Don't rush on regardless, fighting to make it to the top in the fastest in time this century. If you do you will miss it. And that would be a shame. The trees on the upper heights of Mt. Misery are unique. They grow in eternal cloud and have to resist the full force of the trade winds, up where they are strongest. They are twisted and stunted. They appear tortured beyond the definition of the word, tree. At first, you shudder in horror thinking you are seeing the handiwork of some devil from hell.

But after a while, after seeing tree after tree twisted and torn each in a different way, you start to see a beauty in their endurance. Mile after mile, yard after yard, you climb higher and higher, your legs in pain. Each foot in elevation results in even more deformed trees. As you reach for the peak, still believing the signs promising beauty down in Bottom, you start to admire the endurance of such trees. Of what they had to endure, of what torture they had gone through just to survive. On the top, I don't want to relate the non-photo opportunity. Or how I cursed.

It is a long way down, too. And going down you don't have the lure of a photo opportunity giving you strength for the next step. On each step, your eyes are again try to make sense of this mishmash of tree like growth, and you start to feel you are in some kind of church. A church honoring the spirit of life. Honoring the struggle against impossible odds.

By the time you reach the bottom of the mountain you will find yourself begging the trees to teach you how to live and not give up. How to fight even if you have to alter yourself just to survive. You will see the trees in a new light. Towards the bottom the trees will start to seem the most beautiful plant you have ever seen. You will wonder why you have a photo of a tall, straight redwood on a wall of your house. What is so beautiful about that? That tree had it easy.

Mt. Misery will teach you about the beauty of struggle, and you will sail away from Saba a changed person. A person less shallow. A person less vain. A person more likely to see a beggar on a street and nod at him in recognition of his struggle to survive and knowing now, after Saba, that you are looking at yourself before you die. The struggle of pain you will go through. Knowing now, that life is never easy.

Is that what Adam and Eve saw after eating of the Tree of Knowledge? That an Eden is a place for visiting but not for living in?

EXUMAS
BAHAMAS
ATLANTIC OCEAN

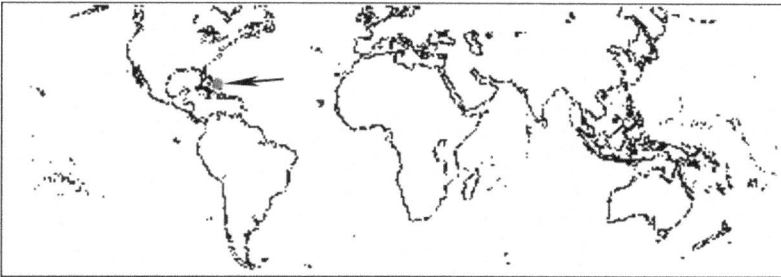

The Bahamas resemble Ant so much that it is scary. Isn't an eden supposed to take years of struggle to reach? But here are the Bahamas just 43 nautical miles from a major American city and somehow, someway they still haven't lost their eden-ness. 700 islands and only 30 are inhabited, that sounds like a possible eden right off, doesn't it? There is no need for a vote because everyone agrees, the Exumas are the queen of the Bahamas. 365 islands spread southward for 145 miles and you are never even faintly out of sight of land. Often dozens of islands can be seen at the same time and almost everyone lives on just two islands. Sailors have been visiting the Exumas for centuries and still they are beautiful. Still you can jump in the water and come up with dinner in just a few minutes. Still the only inhabitants of 98% of the islands are birds, hermit crabs and iguanas. Still you can rig a hammock between two coconut trees and no one will bother you for months at a time. Still the water defies description it is so clear. Still at times you can't say for sure where the sky stops and the water begins. The Exumas are a paradise.

So what if they want hundreds of dollars for a cruising permit. Do you know how much diesel you will burn and gear you will break trying to get to Ant or Chagos or Middle Percy? What more can I say? I certainly am not going to ruin your experience by telling which cays I prefer. Visit them all and decide for yourself. They are all beautiful. They are a shining arc of unique pearls just waiting for your visit.

Yes, Georgetown is crowded, often ridiculously so. Pick up your supplies and move on. Or if you feel like socializing for a few weeks, meeting some of the boats heading in the same direction as you, comparing experiences, sharing pot lucks, then do it. Even Adam got lonely in his Eden! When you have had enough, the Out Islands are just a day sail away. How could life be so perfect?

Why on earth are you still sitting at your marina or anchorage? We are talking about a paradise here! A return to Eden. Go! Go now! Just don't listen to any talking snakes.

BAY OF ISLANDS
NEW ZEALAND
PACIFIC ISLANDS

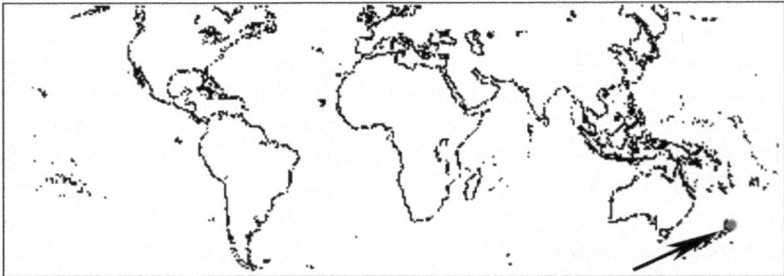

I have always had a fascination with New Zealand. Not only is it a beautiful country but it is run like a country should be run. The land is over 500,000,000 years old nevertheless it was the last sizeable piece of land on earth discovered. Polynesians found New Zealand unoccupied in 800 AD as a true paradise. The animals, fish and birds (including the flightless moas, many species of which ranged from turkey size to over 10 feet tall) were innocent of man. There were so many moas and they tasted so good that they fed countless generations of Maori before they became extinct. Why, back then, did humans always destroy edens when they found them? Hopefully we are different now. In this book are many genuine edens. I hope you will not destroy them when you arrive there. I hope you will leave only footprints on the beach where they will be washed away, and take only photos that you will share only with those who will protect Mother Nature. Remember, land developers like to destroy edens.

Today, New Zealand is different and the same. It is still perhaps the most beautiful country on Earth, and while the beauty of the original Land of the Long White Cloud, is long gone, a new beauty has taken its place. This beauty is best displayed in the Bay of Islands. A bay of yachties, of birds, of green lip mussels, of schools of fish that defy counting, of beauty that seeps into your soul and changes you forever.

New Zealanders pride themselves in ensuring they export far more than they import. Rather than import something from overseas, they build it themselves, for themselves. An important part of the beauty of New Zealand and especially the Bay of Islands is the sense of a people still in charge of their own destiny. So many countries have lost this sense and are tossed this way and that by politicians and robber barons.

The Bay of Islands consists of 150 islands in a rather smallish bay. The opening to the sea is 11 miles wide. On entering, green islands sprout up everywhere you look, one after another, after another. Each island teems with shell fish (the BOI Green Lip Mussels are famed throughout the world). Slowly you wend your way through island after island till finally you reach Opua where you check in. Formalities are over within minutes as you were told all the rules in Fiji or Tonga and were letter perfect on arrival. Anchor off Russell where circumnavigators for years have settled when they became too old to fight the sea. Walk around and breathe the air. In every house you see dwell people who have logged more miles than you might ever hope to. Pau Hana (after work) belly up to the bar at the yacht club and listen to the yarns and maybe tell a few yourself. But don't stay there. Sail back to those incredible islands. Explore each. Eat mussels, eat fish, drink those good Kiwi reds. If ever there was a place for a sailor to truly enjoy himself, it is in the BOI. So what exactly are you waiting for? Permission? Ha! You think circumnavigators wait for permission? Hopefully you aren't waiting!

For some unknown reason used cars are dirt cheap on the North Island of New Zealand. For $500 Kiwi you can get a rolling wreck that will take you through some of the most beautiful scenery on earth. Campgrounds dot the country. Pitch your tent under apple trees, next to roaring mountain trout laden streams, and breathe the air of contentment. Contentment is a good word. Is that what edens are all about, being content? Is happiness an excess of contentment? I don't know, I really don't. Maybe the next time I sail into the Bay of Islands I'll figure it out. Maybe you will. Give it a try!

BERMUDA

WESTERN ATLANTIC OCEAN

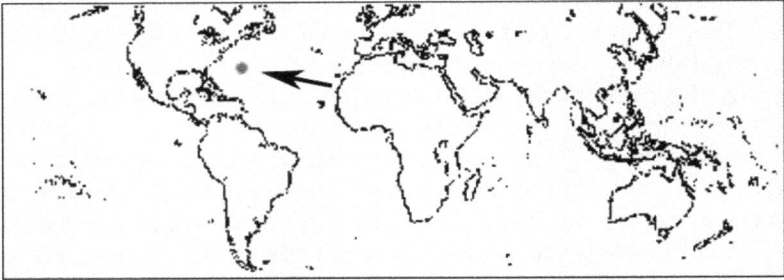

For some reason I always thought that Bermuda was an atoll like group of islands. I knew it had a lot of wind at times and I always hesitated to go there imagining 40 knots of wind howling over a thin piece of reef and on to my boat tugging at the anchor with more reef just behind and me chewing my finger nails to the quick and my ulcer developing minute by minute. Was I ever surprised to get there and have to go through a pass between two tall islands. The pass was so thin the channel markers were on top of the cliff! A tall cliff!

Bermuda is another of those distant lands that remind Englishmen of the mother country. It could easily be a lost piece of England if you ignore the blazing white sand beaches, the warmish water and the lack of fog and incessant rain. It is an archipelago of islands dotted with hills and dales, of quaint shops (sorry, shoppes), of small crofts pretending they are houses, of flowers everywhere and of the politest people on earth. They are! Very, very polite! One of the great things to do in Bermuda is to rent a little 100cc motorbike and zip around and see all the sights. There are only 7 main islands, all connected with bridges, so you can do whatever interests you easily in one day. The roads are very skinny and it is easy to forget that you are supposed to be driving on the left. So there you go, put-putting around the blind curves of hills on the wrong side of the road, going as fast as you can go (which luckily isn't very fast!), only to find a little old man with white hair, driving a Rolls, stopped and patiently waiting for you to be finished with his side of the road. He heard you coming, and knew from experience that you would be on the wrong side. As you guiltily return to your side of the road, he gives you a happy wave as he returns to motoring. No, it isn't just one or two nice people. They all are like that. Amazing!

72

In 1609, 150 British colonists heading for Jamestown were shipwrecked on Bermuda in a fierce storm. Shakespeare wrote 'The Tempest' in memory of the event. The people stayed on and Bermuda was born. Smart people. Bermuda has one of the very highest GNP of any country in the world.

St. George's (on the East End) harbor is as landlocked as it possibly can be without becoming a lake! Hamilton, on the West End, is wide open. On the other hand it is a free port. So that is why we had a motor scooter and why we were driving on the wrong side of the road.

The food is English which means the best you can hope for is fish and chips and boiled veggies. But the people. You will sail on remembering that you don't have to be rude and obnoxious in life. You can be like Bermudians. Exceptionally polite!

In edens there is no need to fight to get ahead or to get the best seat or to get the last apple. Edens are about sharing and smiling and being happy. They are about enjoying life. Once you are in a paradise, there is no need to struggle or to fight. All the tools civilization has instilled within us suddenly become unneeded. They can be discarded, thrown away as useless or at least stashed away in a closet. Are the Bermudians so nice because they don't have to struggle anymore? Is struggling the opposite of heaven?

I know many people who love to struggle. I myself like heavy weather just for the struggle, for the excitement. Is one kind of eden for everybody? Not a chance! That is why there are so many paradises listed within. Take you pick, go out and find your own, start a collection. But whatever you do, don't just sit there and wish you could be happy. Don't live your life hoping paradise is going to come knocking at your door one day. Go out and find it, raise the anchor, hoist the sails, search for new horizons. Is the true happiness the searching for happiness? The pursuit of Happiness?

MT. DESERT ISLAND
MAINE
ATLANTIC OCEAN

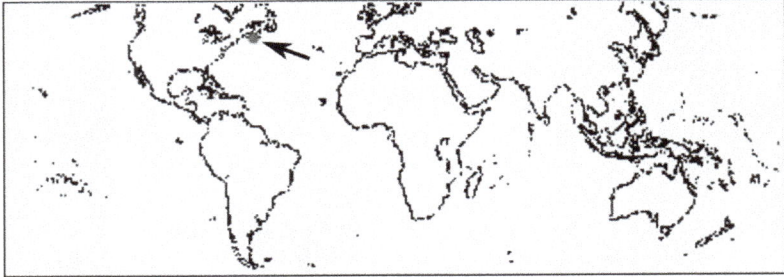

Maine is a great state. Really. Remember, I am a Californian who was born to distrust anything on the East Coast, but I am telling you, when it comes to Edens, it doesn't get much better than Mount Desert, in the summer.

Mount Desert is the home of Arcadia National Park, the first East Coast National Park ever declared, and to some, better than Yellowstone or Sequoia. It hosts Cadillac Mountain, the tallest mountain on the Atlantic Coast north of Rio. Here are some of the advantages of Mt Desert. The bus service all around the island is free and dogs are allowed on board! (It is funded by L.L. Bean) There is no admission fee to the park. There are endless trails, some for horses, some for walking, some for biking, some for just sitting around and gawking at the scenery.

There are towns on Mt Desert. Southwest Harbor is the biggest and the home of Hinckley Yachts, but don't even think of anchoring in the harbor, just grab a mooring and pretend it is yours! Bar Harbor is a waste of time unless you like Waikiki mixed with Jamestown and a bit of New York. But the best isn't a town at all. Somes Sound almost cuts the island in half and at the top of the Sound is one of the most beautiful spots on earth that you can get to by boat. Lots of room to anchor, free showers at the camp sites, (if you want hot water, you have to feed quarters into the meter) beaver, otters, eagles, multitudes of fish, berries in the woods, apples in the trees and a lot of laughing fellow rovers. How can you do better than that?

Everywhere you go in Maine, perfect strangers are asking you to dinner. It is really amazing after the paranoid other 49 States who never talk to strangers. Maybe it is because during the winter there is no one here, or at least no one walking outside. They are hungry for company. Or maybe they are just really nice people! If you go somewhere with grumpy people, damn hard to call it a paradise, isn't it?

The real reason you go to Mt Desert is for the lobsters. Don't you dare go to a restaurant. You can go anywhere in the world and get old, stale lobsters. This is your chance to get lobsters like the Indians and the pilgrims had so many years ago. Here is what you do, just in case you don't know.

Buy your bugs off the lobster boat as he is coming in. He is going to sell them to the factory where they ship out the best lobsters and feed the seconds to the tourists. From the fishermen, a big lobster is $5. Take him home. Pick him up and stand him on his pointy head with his claws balancing him and stroke his tail from the carapace to the small end as you boil the water. Soon he will fall asleep. When the water is at a roiling boil, so it is over quick, gently drop him in. There will be a bit of a fuss but nothing like dropping a green lobster into boiling water with him grabbing the top out of your hands and throwing it about the boat and then climbing out of the pot as mad as hell! He won't take long to cook. Take him out, melt some butter, eat. I know, I know. You never knew lobster could taste like that. Everyone says the same.

Mt. Desert hypnotized green lobsters are the most perfect food on the planet, period, bar none. You have to try them at least once in your life. Don't buy just one. Buy a lot and have a feast. Invite all your friends, new and old. And yes, invite a stranger.

Maybe it is the air up there in Maine. Maybe it is the Mainers who delight in inviting strangers for dinner. Maybe part of paradise is accepting people, untried, as friends, sharing what you have, expecting nothing in return.

How much of paradise is an island or a bay or a harbor? How much of an eden is the way we view the world? Could we travel to a paradise and be unhappy? Never! A true Eden can remake us all!

SINGAPORE
STRAITS OF MALACCA
SOUTH CHINA SEA

I hate to tell anyone reading this who is from a first world country, that you aren't. In a first world country, that is. You are in a second world country. The only first world country in the world today is the city state of Singapore. What Singapore is doing today, the rest of the world is doing tomorrow. I know you don't want to hear it, but it is the sad, scary truth.

Take medical care, for example. Singapore started with the Australian idea that a bloke's wage is a bloke's wage. It doesn't matter what job you do. You should become a doctor because you want to heal people, not because you want to become rich. Doctors and welders are paid the same in Australia. It helps that lawyers are unwelcome in Australia or Singapore. Karen went into for a check for skin cancer. They scanned every inch of her body and burned off 7 evil looking spots within 30 minutes of entering the office, and it cost 50 bucks American, and only that much because they charged ahead for after operation check ups just to be sure that she would come back.

The roads are uncrowded and there are no police in one of the most crowded places on earth. Every car that uses the freeways or the thoroughfares has to have an electronic device that charges you money right out of your bank account if you traveled during the after work rush hour. No charge if you drive 30 minutes later. If you run a red light or cut someone off, your bank account is automatically charged. Parking, need you guess?

Developers building high rises are required to build and fund schools, grocery stores, playgrounds, and monorail stops for every building they erect. Plus they must build 7 times the footprint in parks that their building occupies.

Chewing gum is forbidden as it slows down the monorail system that covers the entire island. But you can live anyway you want, believe anything you desire, work at any job you can think up. There are few taxes. The island runs on fines! Do something wrong, they don't send you to jail, they fine you. Run out of money? Someone has to clean the sewers.

If you ever wanted to visit a country run by Big Brother, or to take a good look at the future, Singapore might just be the eden for you.

If you don't have a problem with authority, like not having cop blowing their sirens at you, enjoy having a free life as long as you don't break the law, maybe Singapore is your eden! Go and find out!

THE SAINTS
SOUTH OF GUADELOUPE
CARIBBEAN SEA

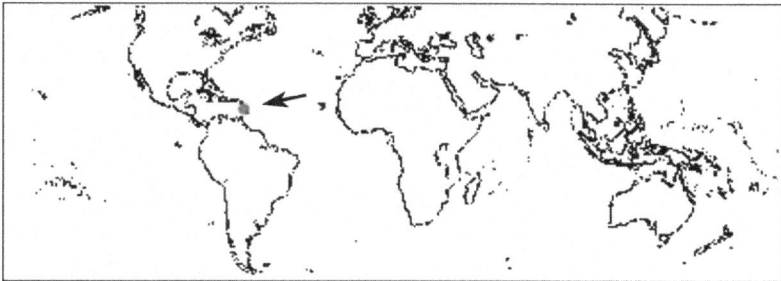

There is no question that the French islands of the Saints are a eden. No question at all. First; they are exquisitely groomed with fruitful fields and orchards, each of the 30 islands and islets is planted with different crops, the buildings could well be from a Paris from a hundred years ago (They might actually have come from there!), and; there are 42 French restaurants on the islands that create the best food in the Caribbean. What am I saying? They may well create the best food in the world outside of Thailand. Definitely better than anything in Paris if only for the scenery. Not a month goes by on the radio nets that someone asks their friends how soon they are leaving the Saints. Their reply is always something like this; "Well, we've been to 18 of the restaurants here, so I figure we will leave in 24 more days." If you are going to go out every night to eat anyway, why not go out for the best food around?

The islands are well protected from the north winds and the northern swell by the bulk of Guadeloupe. The islands themselves are arranged around a central bay to make it a quiet anchorage no matter which restaurant you are visiting tonight. Beautiful trails crisscross the islands guiding you thru fields of wheat, fruit orchards, copses of berries, wild flowers and a stand or two of pumpkin. It is like walking the fields of the south of France but with the glorious trades blowing to keep you cool. Traditionally a sailor should explore an island a day to build up an appetite for the feast coming for dinner in yet another fabulous restaurant. When you have explored the islands, the fishing hereabouts is first rate, and there is always a side trip to Dominica for the veggie markets and the obligatory trip to the waterfalls.

Are the Saints an Eden? If you like to eat well, and you can afford it, The Saints are an experience you will remember and brag about for the rest of your life. So start saving your pennies!

DRY TORTUGAS
FLORIDA
GULF OF MEXICO

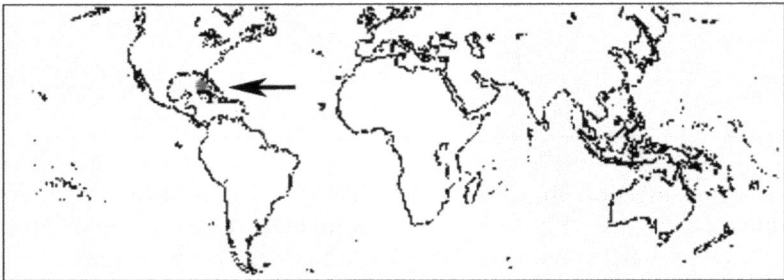

The Dry Tortugas and Fort Jefferson are incredible. There, it is, in print. Now you have to believe it. I know that there are thousands out there who believe that because of the water police, Florida is at the bottom of the list, eden wise. While that might well be true, before you seal your words in concrete, visit Fort Jefferson first. In fact, visit on Thanksgiving day.

Florida doesn't stop at Key West no matter what the city fathers would like us to believe. A whole series of reefs extend westward into the Gulf of Mexico ending in the Dry Tortugas. Here, on Garden Key, the largest all-masonry fort in the Americas was constructed but never finished. It housed confederate prisoners during the American Civil War including Samuel A. Mudd who received a life sentence for setting John Wilkes Booth's broken leg after the assassination of Abraham Lincoln.

It is the caretakers of this park that make this an eden. An eden for one day a year. It is a lonely life out there on the edge of civilization. Their only relief is the rare sailboat that happens their way. On Thanksgiving Day, the Park Rangers prepare a giant roast pig and host a pot luck for anyone who happens to be in the anchorage. What a feast! The yachties bring the side dishes as well as copious amounts of alcohol.

The rest of the year, except for the fishing, the Dry Tortugas are a dusty, sinking (the fort is so heavy it is slowly sinking into the Key), ho hum park. But on that one day it is indeed an Eden! Who are we to ignore edens wherever we can even find them?

HONEYMOON COVE
DAZANTE
BAJA CALIFORNIA, MEXICO

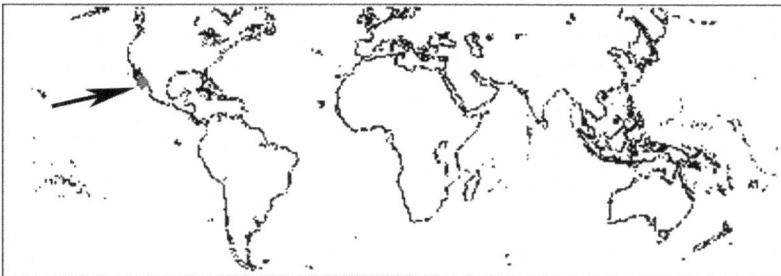

Some places in this old world of ours are still virgin no matter how many times others have anchored there. When you stop, it is like for the first time human prints have trod upon the sands. It is like a true and wonderful discovery, as if you are Columbus discovering a new world. Honeymoon Cove will be a new world to you when you anchor. It is called Honeymoon because the little bay is so narrow only one boat can fit in and then only if she anchors bow and stern. The cove is exquisite. A small sandy beach lies at the head of the cove, just right to make love on. The water is crystal clear and rock scallops line the edges. A series of paths, built by previous honeymooners lead inland guiding you onto new explorations, to new scenic delights. But none of the above is why Honeymoon Cove qualifies as a paradise.

The cove has some strange attraction to sea creatures. It is often visited by spinner dolphin who delight in jumping out of the water in graceful leaps that some observers insist resemble hearts. If a stinky smell comes wafting over your boat at night, it is not your lover's breath, it is a sleeping whale who drifted in with the tide. Huge 6 foot long Humboldt squid strand themselves on the beach for some unknown reason. Don't get too close. Even when dying they have the strength to do you serious harm. Look at them closely and see the intelligence in their eyes. Scary, huh! But sea creatures are not the reason Honeymoon is a paradise.

Look at the smile on your loved one's face as you lie on your private beach all alone. Watch as your honey arcs and writhes in ecstasy while making love. Some places in this world are more conductive to love making than others. Some have some magnetic force or something that encourages romance. Some places give you the energy and stamina to spend the day in each other's arms. And the nights! Lying on the foredeck, bathed by the light of thousands of stars, gazing into each other's eyes. Wow! That alone qualifies Honeymoon Cove worthy as a eden.

Dazante is a gorgeous island, a island of cliffs and spire-like mountains. A land of mystery and adventure, but most of all an island of love, of peace and of quiet. It would be sad if you are ever in the area, to miss this eden. Besides, your loved one will never forgive you for missing the experience!

GALLE
SRI LANKA
INDIAN OCEAN

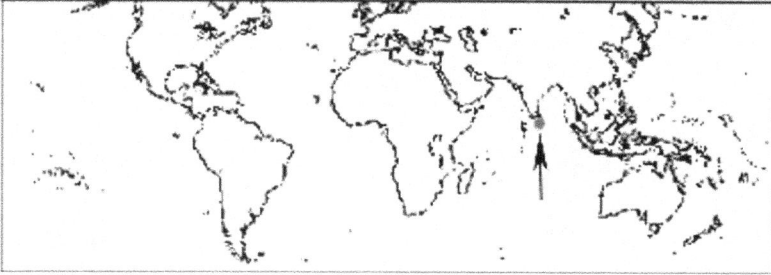

Sri Lanka is an old country. It's continuous history goes back for thousands of years. It is a poor country, however. The streets are filthy, going to the market, while cheap, requires standing in 6" of last week's veggies mixed with mud. The place is famous for its gems. A smart operator can score a truly fabulous stone for pennies on the dollar, but is it worth it? The old harbor, stinks. Often you have to anchor in the outer bay which often rolls unforgivably. Doesn't sound much like an eden, does it?

Dear Reader and Seeker of Paradises, physical beauty sometimes is all that is required to be in the running for an eden. Sometimes, however, other experiences can change you forever. And being changed to the better is definitely a requirement of an eden. Galle is included here solely for one reason. It has perhaps the last true great restaurants of the Victorian Age. Do you remember your history books? Of the huge feasts? Of dish after dish being offered to the dinners for hours every night? Of servants duty bound to cater to the guest's every whim? This way of life still survives to this day. It survives in a particular corner on the old British Empire, Galle.

You sit down at the table and the servants places your napkin on your lap as others bring the rice. In the Orient, rice always comes first. One holds the bowl, the other ladles the rice on to your plate. They would never dream to assume to decide when you have had enough. They will continue to ladle on the rice until it covers the table and the floor and only then stop because you raise your hand, indicating enough. Other servants bring in the meat, then the fish, then the fowl, then the veggies. There is no menu. You sit down and choose what to eat as it is brought out to your nose and eyes. At the same time, still other servants carry in the wine, the rare whiskeys and as desserts approach, the ports and the sherries.

You are pampered beyond belief, beyond anyone in this civilization believes is possible. This is how the upper crust used to live. No wonder that long ago civilization created so many poets and writers, so many adventurers and con men. After a night or a week living like this, with servants washing your back in the tub, combing your hair till is shines, will you be different to? Will you seek to achieve something great, something to prove that you have the right to be in the upper crust of society? Want to find out? Sail into Galle!

DESOLATION SOUND
BRITISH COLOMBIA
PACIFIC OCEAN

I have only visited Desolation once and that was well over 40 years ago but the memories haunt me still. Desolation is a sound lying inside Vancouver Island along the Canadian British Columbian coast. It cuts deep into the land and is surrounded by tall snow topped mountains.

The upper sound ends in a small lake that is blessed with hot springs. This means that the water never freezes over in winter. In the past people spent the winter in Desolation Sound. Strange people who liked their edens laced with solitude. It is different nowadays. Thanks to HF radios, SSB news programs and Ham radio, Desolation is never as lonely as it was before. Now in the winter, writers, philosophers, mathematicians, and of course, hermits purposely ice themselves in and spend the winter in Desolation. It doesn't freeze over in the upper reaches but down by the entrance the ice is many feet thick. A requirement to survival is a wood burning stove. Wood because dead falls can be easily found all winter long so if it is a late year, you won't freeze. But why would people do this to themselves?

Desolation Sound is very likely the last truly pure place on Earth. It is beyond beautiful, beyond spectacular. My favorite memories are of eagles spotting a salmon on the surface and roaring down from a thousand feet, braking at the last second the wind roaring in their feathers sounding like a locomotive. They pull the fish out of the water, often times as big as they are and by pure will power pull it back up the mountain tops, white except in the middle of August. They do the same thing around Chatterbox Falls in Princess Louisa Inlet a few miles south of Desolation. This is a beautiful summertime spot chockablock full of oysters on top of bigger oysters. There is a free dock supplied by the Seattle Cruising Club for those who need their solitude supplied in comfort!

It is warm enough in Desolation for beaver and otter to entertain us all winter. Elk and moose, bear and wolverine come down to look for food and to have a drink. Warm enough for us to brew beer all winter. With only a few hours of light, wild parties are scheduled for the night, some times all night. Great thoughts are shared and instantly forgotten. Friendships are forged and forever remembered. Is Desolation Sound an eden? You bet it is! And I can't wait to go back!

KUMAI
SOUTHERN BORNEO
INDONESIA
JAVA SEA

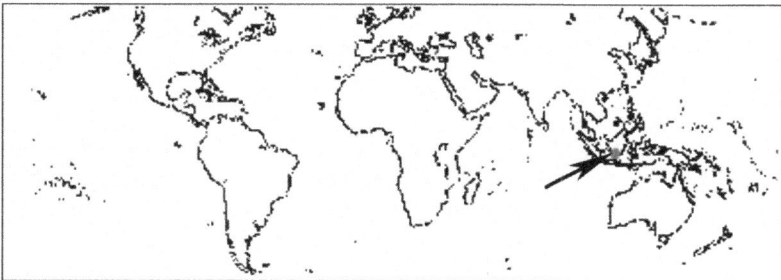

Deep in the wilds of Borneo, away from the disruptions of civilization, is a camp where biologists attempt to reintroduce orangutans to the wild. These apes were captured as babies and placed in bars around the seaports of Southeast Asia. Orangutans share many of the vices of humans, including alcoholism. As a lark, sailors off of merchant and military ships would buy these apes beer which increased the owner's profits. Eventually they become older and more aggressive and start stealing sailors drinks and eventually setting up camp behind the bar and helping themselves. Normally they are killed at this point, but many kind hearted people are trying to reintroduce these apes into the jungle and to prevent the babies from being stolen in the first place. One of these camps is up a river near Kumai.

We went up this river and had the time of our lives. Wild animals were everywhere. We watched troops of monkeys cross crocodile infested rivers. The big males could swing across. The mothers swam across with all their offspring holding on to her back or sitting of her head! At night lightning bugs lit the surrounding trees so brightly we could read by their light! Crocs swam by with giant leaves balanced atop their heads to disguise their intents. Hundreds of species of birds flew this way and that. We had the best time. Zoos are depressing in a way with their cages and bored animals. Not like on this river trip! What a blast! After a couple days of enchantment we reached the orangutan camp many miles up river.

They liked to hang out by the river still hoping for a sailor to give them a beer. We were told it was incredibility dangerous to do so. The apes would fight over it and trample us in the melee. Instead, they tried to make friends with us. One big girl took a shining to me after she slid her hand down my front pocket to be sure I was sufficiently endowed! The apes were fed many miles inland to get the orangutans used to the jungle. We walked in, carrying little babies in our arms. Once there, big silverbacks swung into the feed station to eat first as was their custom. What beautiful animals in the wild! How sad we only see them in zoos where all the fire is extinguished from their eyes and they sit around instead swinging their 700 pound bodies across huge open spaces with 2 fingers!

If wild animals are part of your eden, this is the place you belong. Some yachties are so entranced, they tie up their boats and spend months up the river. Maybe you will too! They are always looking for volunteers. Maybe you could write a book about it?

GOA
INDIA
ARABIAN SEA

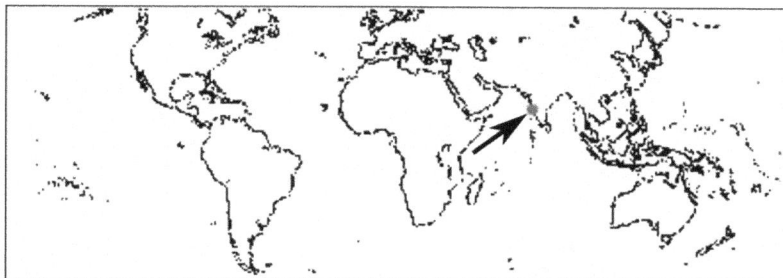

Goa is not ancient like Galle. Nothing of the old Hindu city of Goa remains. Portugal seized Goa back when and made it into the capitol of their vast Eastern territories. By 1575, everything about the city was Portuguese. In 1962, India took Goa back but it was too late. It still remains a European city run by Indians. What does this mean to us paradise hunters?

At one time, Goa was the eden of the European jet set. They went there for vacant, endless beaches, cheap drugs and a then weird philosophy. India stopped the drugs (at least the cheap ones!), the philosophy became less weird but the beaches are still there. However, to cater to the jet set, many beach restaurants were built. These are still there, too. The food is wonderful, cheap and hot. Yes, hot from the oven, but spicy, too.

If you don't like curry, stop reading! The only good food in India that doesn't have curry in it, is pound cake. They do make great cakes but could you survive on it?

At these restaurants, when you order an omelet, often a chicken thigh and a piece of liver comes with it, all for a dollar! (1987 dollar!) And they give you the first beer for free. Goa has retained its right, unlike the rest of India, to sell alcohol freely.

So if you are in the area, and looking for a beach eden, go to Goa. Yes, they will sell you tons of trinkets and stare at you for hours. But the beach restaurants are worth it. Plus if you are still looking for a weird philosophy, once a decade they take Saint Francis Xavier's body on a trip around town. His body never decayed, it looks like he is just sleeping. Now is that weird or what?

TANGA
TANZANIA
INDIAN OCEAN

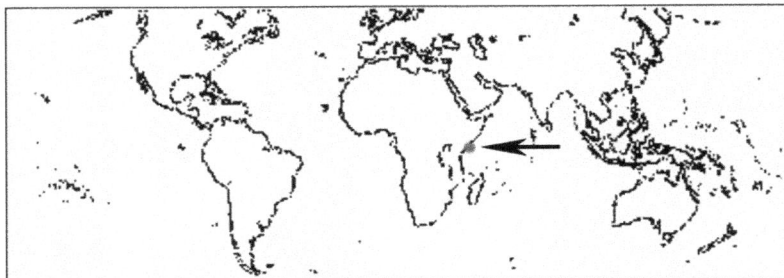

Tanga is one of the last old time Arab ports in the world. It is a well protected port with jagged coral reefs lining the only channel making the entrance hair raising. You get in and anchor just around the point from the entrance and then stare in amazement as huge 70 foot dhows follow you in with the wind drumming in their huge lateen sails hung from 100 foot masts. They race through the entrance to keep their maneuverability at its highest and then once inside, drop their sails and glide, with only their momentum as forward force, the mile to the old docks. As they pass, your body shakes with the roar of their luffing sails and your feet tap along with their Arabic chanteys that they sing as they work their boat. What an introduction to Africa!

Many expatriates come down to the yacht club. They might have spent years in the wop wops running plantations, the only white man for hundreds of miles surrounded by a hundred thousand blacks. The stories they tell as we sit in the yacht club drinking our ice cold beer. I wonder why I once thought the age of wooden ships and iron men was gone. I saw one of them in town when a mini riot had started over some silly thing. He walked right into the middle of a thousand blacks, each twice his size, and dominated the situation with just the force of his personality and the molten iron in his will and eyes.

One of them took us for a local's safari. He was going up country and he let us follow along in his backseat. The first night we were surrounded by hundreds of elephants knocking trees down to eat the tops, and us sleeping in little 2 man tents. Karen and I were fairly freaked until he stuck his head into our tent.

"Can't little things like this disturb you. Elephants hardly ever step on tents. Relax. It isn't like they are lions." That was a great big help, believe me! The next day he took us to see some feeding lions, blood squirting out as they killed, the immense strength as they carried their prey behind some rocks to dine in peace. Karen stuck her upper body out of the window trying to get a better photo. Our guide finally freaked out and bodily pulled Karen back in. He pointed to the feeding lions. "Those are lionesses. The lion is around here somewhere, probably within 10 meters of this car. He protects the pride as they feed. If he attacks, you will be dead before you see him. They are very, very fast, never put your body out of the car next to a kill. Never." Karen nodded mutely, her skin ashen. A minute later a huge lion stuck his head out from around a bush 10 feet away and licked his chops while staring into Karen's shocked eyes!

The East Coast of central Africa is rampart with sharks. Dead bodies are routinely thrown in the harbor as an easy burial. Nevertheless, it is a Sunday tradition to have a picnic on a sandbar just outside the harbor. Starting at low tide, wearing tuxedos and fancy dresses the long time African hands would set up tables and chairs and feast away until the tide threatened to carry away their tables. Only then would they reluctantly board their launches and head back to the club kicking away the odd inquisitive shark.

Spitting cobras are common in this part of the world. They are deadly aimers and can spit a vicious poison into the eyes of anyone they dislike, blinding them for hours. Those blinded, they bite and kill. They only eat the sexual organs of the males. The old hands discovered that German Shepard's are immune to the poison and being active aggressive dogs, have little trouble keeping the spitting cobra population down.

If your eden includes meeting men who are fearless and capable, go to Tanga. This is your town. Here there be, not dragons, but dragon slayers! They might just sweep you off your feet, girls! Men, do you want to develop a real 1000 yard stare? Places like Tanga are getting rarer and rarer. See one before it is too late.

Is Tanga an eden? What to you want to do in paradise? Sit around and stare into your belly button? Live your life to the fullest. Pull into Tanga! Be all that you can be!

RUSSIAN BAY
MADAGASCAR
INDIAN OCEAN

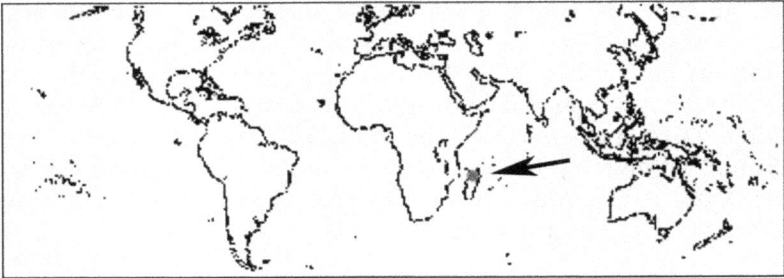

I love Madagascar! It is so dark and yet it is full of light. Filled with the darkest of jungles, populated with the clearest eyes and untroubled brows you are ever likely to see. The best cruising is in the north, next to Nosy Be. This island with the funny name is one of those places that only the French seem able to develop. It is full of vineyards and wheat fields, owned by locals speaking French. It could be a paradise, but only if you are fluent in French. For the rest of us, a little bay 20 miles to the south is the real thing. An absolute Eden, with a capital E.

A few years ago, a Russian war ship decided they had enough of the USSR and defected. But they didn't want anyone to get their ship. They weren't traitors, they just wanted to be free. So they sailed to Madagascar, found a beautiful bay, blew up their ship, Bounty style, and settled down to live with the locals in happiness and joy sure that the Russian Navy would give up looking for them after a few years. They didn't. After ten years the Navy found them, seized the mutineers, grabbed all the half cast descendents they could find and brought them back to Russia to be adopted. Since then the bay has been considered bad luck to the locals and is left to be enjoyed by the yachties. And it is great!

Huge trees bend their branches down like weeping willows creating living tents on the beach, but tents 100 foot across. Inside, the Russians left tables and chairs made out of rocks, fireplaces too and piped water to flow under the trees and out to the ocean. Fruit trees are everywhere for your pleasure, at least they are if you can beat the lemurs to the fruit! The fishing is unbelievable. Huge fish jump onto the deck of your boat. Absolutely true! Who needs a hook and line?

Sail a little way north or south and the locals come out of hidden passes in the dark seemingly impassable forest to trade fruit and veggies with you for old tee shirts. Honey River, 15 miles to the south, just makes honey. That is all they do. A dollar a liter and that is a tourist price! You do have to supply you own container.

Have a potluck at night on the beach and listen to the untamed jungle at your back. Listen to the birds, to the insects, to the lemurs, to who knows what that was. Remember that this is what we have descended from, that you are listening to your own roots. Does it send a shiver down your spine? Do the hormones deep in your blood throb a bit more powerfully?

Is Russian Bay an eden? Some say they can hear voices at night of children being torn from the arms of their mothers. But I am sure they are imagining it, at least I hope so! Ghost stories aside, Russian Bay is one of the most premier paradises in this book. Circle it twice in your atlas! Maybe three times!

KO MUC
PHANG NA BAY
EAST OF PHUKET
BAY OF BENGAL, INDIAN OCEAN

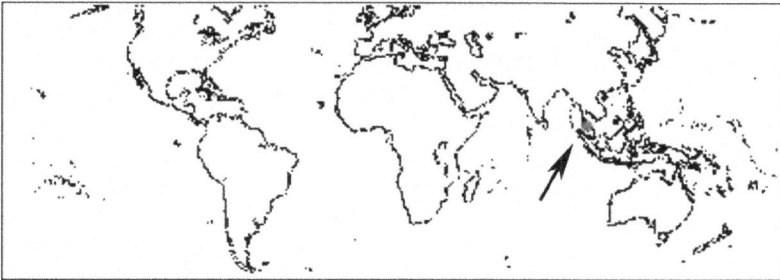

Ko Muc is a hong. No doubt that doesn't mean much to you. Hongs start as deep caves that develop in basaltic rock islands, then the middle of the island caves in from lack of support leaving perhaps the most remarkable land formation on Earth, a hong. It is a roofless cave that is still reached through long thin tunnels from the sides. Ko Muc is the most fabulous hong ever discovered. It is unbelievable that no one is sitting outside charging money. Course, if they did, it wouldn't qualify as paradise material. But they don't and it does, and this one will blow your mind! (If you want to know more about Hongs, I once wrote a Cruising Guide to the Hongs of Thailand. Check Kindle. "The Hong Book")

Approach the western side of Ko Muc at low tide if this is your first time. Look for a little dark hole half out of the water. You can paddle your dinghy in safely if you have practiced paddling side by side. Otherwise, anchor outside and swim in. The tunnel has a sandy bottom and the sides are clear of ouch making animals and rocks. It is quite a ways and the tunnel twists but by the time you lose the light behind you, the light in front comes into view. Don't chicken out.

This is going to be perhaps the most remarkable experience of your life.

When you come out of the tunnel into the once main cave before its top fell down, the first thing you notice are the straight walls going up hundreds of feet, covered with vines, small trees, flowers by the hundreds, nay thousands. Your eye travels to the base of the walls, in front of you and you gasp. There is no way to stop your eyes from bugging out of your head. Ahead of you is the most magnificent beach ever created. Pure white sand is backed by coconut trees leaning over to brush the calm water. It has to be calm, as you are for all practicalities, in a cave. The flowers have continued down their waterfall, on to the floor and are joined by a papaya tree, a mango tree and pineapple bushes. You lay down on the sand. Wait, you strip off every bit of clothing on your body, (no one is there but your honey, right?) then lie down and look up. A telescope of flowers teases your eyes upwards to watch fluffy clouds gently dance their way past your cave top. The sun shines down and you work on your tan as the clouds entrance you into dreams.

Eventually you wake up and go for a swim. Then eat some fruit. Dig your toes into the sand just under the water at low tide and shout in joy when you find the best tasting clams in the world. Make love and sleep again under the now darkening sky. It doesn't get cold. The tall walls of stone radiate their heat and you sleep in comfort, arms around each other. The next morning, the sun will wake you early. Don't hide your eyes. Open them wide. As the sun rises and gently touches the cave walls each petal opens to the warmth of the sun. Inch by inch, soon the entire wall is bursting with color. Eat a fresh breakfast, straight from a tree. Spend the day, relaxed, doing what God intended, naming the flowers and birds.

With a sigh of regret you realize that the boat is all alone anchored out of sight. Time to do your duty and sadly you turn your back and swim out of the tunnel. Back on the boat, you pick up a book and then throw it down again. You pick up the dividers and mark down how far it is to the next island. Sick to your stomach, you throw the dividers down. Finally, the two of you look at each other and nod. Jump in the dinghy and soon you are back in Eden. And it is an Eden. You might spend a month anchored off this hong. I know Karen and I did. But eventually you will have to leave. E-mail, banks, family and friends are tugging too strongly.

But don't worry. You will always carry the peace you found in Ko Muc with you for the rest of your days. Soon you will find it changed you. You are less argumentative, fight less with your spouse, and if you do, if either of you look at the other with that special 'Let's go back to Ko Muc' look, the two of you will fall into each others arms and cry out for your paradise lost. But then as you gaze at each other, in the back of the other's eyes, you can see a dim echo of Ko Muc and happiness and joy you found there return again to bless you until your dying day.

CORONADO
SAN DIEGO BAY
CALIFORNIA
PACIFIC OCEAN

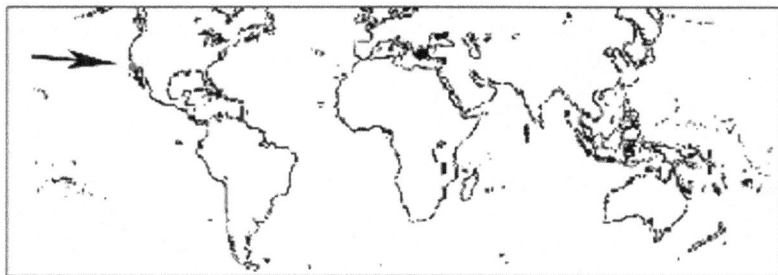

There are a lot of reasons that Coronado Island should not be rated as a cruising paradise. There is a maximum 3 day limit on anchoring in Glorietta Bay, the premier anchoring destination in San Diego. Coronado has become much more crowded than when I was born there so many years ago and traffic is a major problem. There is no need for an alarm clock with 20,000 cars driving over the bridge every morning to go to work in North Island. But there still is something about Coronado that makes it unique among this collection of the greatest islands and edens in the world.

Years ago, California was renown as the last bastion of a gentile civilization. People were nice to each other, really. People stopped on the sidewalks to speak to each other, not friends but perfect strangers. It was a State that prided itself on developing joy, understanding and compassion. That is all gone now. There have been too many immigrants, too many newcomers seeking the proverbial pot of gold, little understanding that the Golden State's uniqueness was within the hearts of its citizens, not buried in the ground. If you missed out, if you never visited California in its golden age, if you are seeking a true Shangri-la but know that it is really difficult to anchor in the middle of the Himalayas, fear not. A little island off the coast of San Diego still retains the joy and friendliness of what once was, the Eden of Coronado.

To someone who hasn't experienced a joyful populace it is next to impossible to describe. But, describing is what authors do best so here goes. Imagine walking down the street and each and every person you pass meets your eyes and smiles. Imagine every other person you meet stops and complements you on your hair or clothes or the often perfect weather. Names are not exchanged. Names are not important. The only thing of importance is the joy in your heart and the fact that you are willing to share it. Imagine meeting a friend on the street and both of you light up with happiness as you approach each other. Yes, yesterday you saw each other, but this is a new day, a day full of possibilities of joy. You land your dinghy on one of the many golden beaches and stroll up the road to the grocery store. Strangers stop and offer you a ride, locals smile as you pass, welcome to Coronado, the last bastion of what was once California.

Coronado has been like this for so many years that the beginnings are lost in antiquity. Perhaps it was first noticed when the Hotel del Coronado was built in 1888 on a sand bar called Coronado outside the harbor of San Diego. The developers looked all over the country for the perfect place to build the greatest hotel of its time. A place that oozed happiness and contentment, where busy men could finally relax for a time. They picked Coronado. They picked it for the beach, arguably in the top ten in America, but mostly they picked it for the atmosphere. In its time the Hotel was occupied by many American Presidents and scores of foreign leaders. All came for the peace and joy the sands extruded.

Should you anchor and experience the 'Island of Enchantment'? Being native born I should say, "Stay Away." But being native born I do say, "Come. Join. It is like no place on Earth."

AFTERWARDS

There is nothing more noble in a life than seeking a better place to live. If you are out here cruising you most certainly have the genes of the pioneers in your chromosomes. The ones that urged them to seek new and better lands.

Don't believe those who say you are just an escapist. They lie! They are just jealous! We aren't running away, we are running towards a new, better and more wonderful life. A life of adventure, of challenge, of joy and of happiness. Those who stay behind wish they were us. Maybe one day they will follow in our wakes and finally find a happiness of their own.

Paradises do still exist in this old world of ours. They always have. But they don't advertise in the Sunday paper or fly flags overhead indicating the parking spaces. You have to find them. It is a quest like the knights of old except instead of dragons, we have our own fears to conquer. Some of these Edens will change you when you find them. Seeking for these Paradises will most definitely change you, for the better.

So, decide. Are you going to stay in the marina or anchored off it? Maybe you can't leave because of family, or the house needs work or you might not have saved enough money. Are you really happy with your present life?

Or are you going to reach out to far horizons and happiness that you have to earn with the love in your heart and the iron in your will. It is up to you. It is your choice. It always has been, you know. Well, what is it going to be? Decide.

OTHER BOOKS BY MIKE RILEY

AVAILABLE AT AMAZON.COM

EDUCATION OF A FALCON
HOW TO *THRIVE* ON A TROPICAL DESERTED ISLAND
THE CORDON ROUGE COOKBOOK
EDENS I HAVE KNOWN AND LOVED
THE TREASURES OF COCOS ISLAND
THE GOOD, THE BAD, AND THE PIRATE
BOAT IMPROVEMENT IN EXOTIC PORTS AROUND THE WORLD

AVAILABLE ON KINDLE

THE GOOD, THE BAD, AND THE PIRATE
THE TREASURES OF COCOS ISLAND
THE HONG BOOK
THE TIGERS WILL EAT YOU ALIVE
BOAT IMPROVEMENT IN EXOTIC PORTS AROUND THE WORLD
HOW TO TIME YOUR SEWING MACHINE

I still publish all my books onboard "Beau Soleil" find me and I'll sell you some. To tell you the truth, Kindle is cheaper! Of course, buy from me and I'll sign them! Soon as I die off, they'll be worth some real money!